PUGLIA

TRAVEL GUIDE

Are You Ready to Visit Southern Italy?

Discover the Best Places of This Wonderful Region
Following the Advice of an Apulian Native,
and Don't Miss Its Incredible Typical Flavors

EXPLORE
Puglia

Get ready for some amazing adventures in Apulia that I've personally collected just for you!

From mouthwatering local delicacies to exploring charming towns and soaking up the sun on stunning beaches, we've got it all covered.

Let's dive into the fun and excitement that awaits you in this fantastic region of Italy. Get set for a blast in Apulia!

Don't miss out! Scan the QR code and let the adventure begin!

Let's make unforgettable memories in Apulia!

SCAN ME

▼

CONTENTS

A FREE BONUS GUIDE
FOR YOU!

- ✓ The Best High-Level Restaurants
- ✓ 7 Itineraries selected by a true Apulian
- ✓ The Most beautiful experiences
- ✓ The 20 must have items you must pack!
- ✓ The Tastiest Wines

Scan this QR and download now your FREE BONUS!

LEAVE A
1 CLICK
REVIEW

Customer reviews

★★★★★ 4.9 out of 5

223 global ratings

5 star		93%
4 star		7%
3 star		0%
2 star		0%
1 star		0%

⌄ How customer reviews and ratings work

Review this product

Share your thoughts with other customers

Write a customer review

SCAN THIS QR
TO GET TO THE
BOOK FASTER

I would be incredibly thankful if you could take just 60 seconds to write a brief review on Amazon, even if it's just a few sentences!

ABOUT FRANCESCO

Hello to you who have this book in your hands and are probably planning to come and visit my beloved Puglia!

Before I leave you to read, I wanted to introduce myself: my name is Francesco Giampetruzzi, known to my friends as "Petrù", I live in Puglia, and I am 26 years old.

I am a farmer with over 7000 trees, including olive, almond, and many other types of fruits, but I also have a passion for traveling and welcoming tourists from all over the world. In particular, Finland kidnapped my heart and continues to kidnap it whenever I return.

But as much as I adore Finland, my love for the land where I was born remains indescribable. I live in the center of many of Puglia's beauties, such as Polignano a Mare, Alberobello, Castellana Grotte, Matera, Monopoli, Bari, Ostuni, Locorotondo, and many other towns full of history, culture, and traditions that, besides me, tourists love!

In addition, the food we produce here has something extraordinary: genuine, high-quality, farm-to-table flavors and ingredients with exceptional properties conferred by the land, sea, and wind of this region, which I would very much like you to taste.

Therefore, after sending dozens of boxes to Finland for my friends to discover Apulian products, I decided to create a box full of delicious foods from my land!

Why did I do all this?

I aim to become your Apulian friend from Italy and show you all the wonders of Puglia through its unique cuisine and places.

But let's go back to the book you are about to read.

Now that you are planning to visit Puglia, I must warn you that you are getting into a lot of trouble: it will not be easy at all to choose what to visit among the hundreds of wonderful places Puglia has to offer.

That's why I created this guide, which will help you decide which stops to include in your Puglia tour and how to organize your itinerary!

As mentioned above, I love welcoming tourists from all over the world, so if you ever need help visiting Puglia, I suggest you check out my site.

You may decide to let an authentic Apulian guide you to discover the most beautiful places in my country!

Now it is time for us to immerse ourselves in a journey among the beauties of my Puglia, so I wish you a fantastic read, with the hope of seeing you here soon!

A hug, Francesco

INTRODUCTION

How beautiful is Puglia?

Answering this question is not difficult at all: Puglia is truly beautiful.

Indeed, according to national and international news outlets, Puglia is so beautiful that it is considered one of the most beautiful regions in the world.

But before we delve into the sumptuous magnificence of this region, let us say right away where it is located.

Puglia is a region of Italy located in its easternmost part in the south. It is a peninsula, washed by the Adriatic Sea in the East and the Ionian Sea in its southwestern part. It is bordered by the Basilicata, Molise, and Campania regions. Its population is about 4 million.

Man's presence in the region has been attested since the Stone Age, as evidenced by the numerous artifacts and findings throughout its territory. In some areas, there are even footprints and fossils testifying to the presence of dinosaurs.

Apulia has always played an important role, not only in the history of Italy but also in Europe, as a real bridge to the East. To go eastward, it was necessary to start from the ports of Apulia; to return from the East, the nearest and obligatory landing place was only one, Apulia.

The comings and goings of people, goods, information, and ideas has dramatically influenced the Apulian territory in every aspect. The succession of Greeks, Romans, Byzantines, Normans, French, Arabs and many other peoples helped create, century after century, an extremely rich, layered, vibrant, and, above all, living culture and tradition. As a result, even today the region maintains its role as a bridge to the East.

In this book, the intent is to capture the essence of Puglia encapsulated in its inhabitants, in their customs, in an area that manifests its beauty in different forms, in its food, in its traditions, and in its history.

In fact, it would be necessary to describe every single aspect of this fantastic region.

I could also just talk about its coast, which stretches for hundreds of kilometers hiding wonderful natural spectacles within every bay and inlet; or about its hinterland, with its woods, forests, natural areas, such as the Murgia and its particular conformation, within which rock civilizations have thrived. Or again, of Apulian gastronomy, which has taken the traditional elements of its cuisine and further enhanced them: bread, oil, cultivated products, and those that grow wild, making Apulia a veritable treasure trove of tastes and flavors.

Take as an example Apulian viticulture, which has been attested to since ancient times.

It was overshadowed by the rest of Italy for a long time, using wines produced in Puglia to "cut" Italian wines, meaning they were used to give body and color to wines from other areas of Italy and Europe.

For the past few decades, however, Apulian winemakers have put all their strengths into bringing Apulian wines to the forefront. They are now known for their quality and are exported worldwide. Red wines, white wines, rosé wines... Puglia is now among the leading areas of quality wine production.

We could also talk about the great religious devotion of this region, manifested in its churches and its rituals related to Christmas, Holy Week and many other religious holidays.

Even more surprising is how the landscape within it, whether historical, natural or gastronomic, is extremely varied, complex, and rich even though the region nevertheless has its common identity character, which makes it immediately distinguishable to those from outside.

In order not to dwell too long and start this journey among Apulian wonders, let us say that Apulia has as many as four sites considered UNESCO World Heritage Sites, with two more "intangible" sites that are candidates to be so in the coming years.

To add more would be useless. So let us end this introduction with a phrase from Emperor Frederick II of Swabia, who loved and gave so much to this region:

> ❝It is evident that the God OF the Jews did not know Apulia and Capitanata. Otherwise He would not have given His people Palestine as the Promised Land.❞

CHAPTER 1

THE
PUGLIA
REGION

To reveal Puglia to you reading this book, I will start with the natural areas that will leave you spellbound.

Let's start by specifying that Apulia can be divided into 6 main natural areas:

1. The Gargano area: located in the north of the region, with its beautiful beaches, Umbra Forest, and the islands of Lesina and Varano;
2. The central Adriatic coast, with the regional capital and beautiful coastal towns full of life and history;
3. The Murgia area: a vast area that includes incredible villages with centuries-old history, culture, and culinary traditions and beautiful landscapes;
4. Itria Valley area, the Trulli area: in this incredible area next to the Trulli (typical world-famous local stone dwellings), you will come across fairy-tale landscapes, as well as taste truly unique traditional products;
5. The Salento area: the Salento peninsula is famous everywhere for its clear waters, coastline, local produce, and festive atmosphere 365 days a year.
6. The Doric-derived city of Taranto and its hinterland that seems like an enchanted world.

Although not part of the region, we can consider the city of Matera and its surroundings as part of the Murgia itinerary.

Matera is a unique city in the world, thanks to the so-called "sassi", rock dwellings directly dug into the rock thousands of years ago. It is enough to think that this is where lived the third oldest civilization ever existed, dating back more than ten thousand years.

It has entered the UNESCO list of World Heritage Sites and today is a destination for tourists worldwide. Here the presence of the peasant civilization is still very strong, and you can still feel it in the narrow alleys that characterize the old part of the city.

DISCLAIMER: As mentioned earlier, this guide does not claim to be exhaustive and complete about all the beauties of Puglia. However, I will try to indicate what is from my experience that I was born and have lived in Puglia all my life, the best itinerary among the many possible of this magnificent region and the different areas that make it up.

GARGANO AREA

The Gargano area encompasses the entire northern part of Apulia: towards the east, there are many beautiful and characteristic coastal villages, set among rocks and headlands, inlets and sea caves, while continuing inland, the terrain becomes more mountainous, and villages settle on hilltops or in the woods. We move from the Adriatic Sea to an area where

we can already smell the scent of mountains because the chain of the Apennines is not far away. The great Umbra Forest is a magnificent and impervious place between the two parts.

MARGHERITA DI SAVOIA AND THE SALT PANS

Among the most interesting areas in the entire northern part of Puglia is the town of Margherita di Savoia, with its salt pans (the largest in Europe) and the whole area attached to them, whose ecosystem has been placed under protection (the so-called wetland). In fact, the site has quite unique characteristics compared to the surrounding area, and over time it has been colonized by pink flamingos. These magnificent birds contribute to the spectacular nature of this place.

But it is not only flamingos that inhabit this area. Indeed, the whole park is a reference point for several species of birds, both migratory and resident.

SOME HISTORICAL BACKGROUND

Margherita di Savoia and its salt pans have recorded human presence since ancient times.

Abandoned at a specific time as a malarial area, from the 17th century, it underwent a gradual process of re-foundation and continuous expansion until its 20th-century industrialization, extending to the point of being the first salt marsh in Europe both in terms of extension and salt production.

Precisely to understand this development, there is a museum dedicated to the salt marshes and their history; meetings, special projects, and guided tours are often organized to learn about the relevance and secrets of this entire so important area.

Read more:

http://www.museosalina.it/il-museo.html

HOW TO VISIT THE SALT PANS AND NATURE PARK

Both the salt pans and the wetland can be visited, with prior reservation at info@salinamargheritadisavoia.it, or at the telephone number 0883 657519.

The salt pans can be visited year-round. However, different types of tours are arranged depending on the season (trekking or bicycle tours are also provided in summer). Whichever type of tour you choose, the presence of a guide is mandatory. It will take you between the salt mining areas and the nature area, explaining how the process takes place, up to the large and impressive salt mountain, the collection point.

You can also do birdwatching activities: in addition to pink flamingos, the area is considered a protected area that hosts more than 200 species of birds, some of whom are endangered. However, even for this type of activity, it is necessary to make reservations and be directed by a guide.

Also linked to salt mining are other types of activities, such as the world-famous thermal baths of Margherita di Savoia.

THE THERMAL BATHS OF MARGARET OF SAVOY

The Thermal Baths of Margherita di Savoia is a spa complex located in the town of Margherita di Savoia. The thermal complex makes use of sulfur waters from the area, which have proven useful in treating a variety of health problems, including skin diseases, respiratory and rheumatic problems. The thermal waters are rich in sulfates, chlorides, bicarbonates and calcium, which are useful in alleviating a variety of ailments.

The spa complex includes swimming pools, saunas, steam baths, and beauty and beauty treatments. In addition, the Margherita di Savoia Thermal Baths also offer rehabilitation and physical therapy programs for patients with injuries or chronic diseases.

The thermal complex also has several facilities to accommodate visitors, including single and double rooms, apartments, and vacation homes. Restaurants, bars, stores and entertainment services are available for visitors. They are open year-round and offer customized treatment packages to meet the needs of anyone who intends to stay here It goes without saying that these spas do not only have a "curative" function; people also come here to relax and enjoy a few hours of pure tranquility, useful for regenerating themselves from the toils of everyday life.

VIESTE AND ITS WONDERFUL BEACHES

Vieste is a coastal town located at the easternmost part of the Gargano promontory. It is known for its natural beauty, particularly its 30 km of unspoiled beach, sea caves (which can be visited by boat), reefs and varied wildlife. The town sits on a peninsula and overlooks the Adriatic Sea, surrounded by a series of bays and inlets, with a crystal-clear sea and sandy and rocky beaches.

But Vieste is not just about nature; the town's historic center attracts tourists with numerous churches and historic buildings, including the Swabian Castle and the Cathedral of Santa Maria di Merino. In a special way, the old part of town

is distinguished by its narrow, winding streets with white houses and red roofs, interspersed with beautiful small squares and courtyards.

To this we add the excellent local food, including vegetables and fresh fish, the very lively nightlife and a series of shows and events that make Vieste a must-visit tourist hub.

We have already mentioned how renowned and famous the beaches of Vieste are, sandwiched between coves and beautiful landscapes, some hidden, others a destination for mass tourism. Let's try to list the best-known ones.

THE CASTLE BEACH

It is Vieste's most famous beach, thanks to its golden-white sand and a seabed that gently slopes into the sea. It lies south of the town and is greeted by the first Gargano sun. There are numerous access points on the Enrico Mattei promenade, making it easy for anyone to enter. It has modern bathing establishments and areas of free beach. The area is equipped with accommodations, restaurants, bars and discos. "Guarding" the beach are the Swabian Castle and the "Pizzomunno" monolith (which we discuss in the paragraph below), a symbol of the town, linked to a legend of sailors in love and jealous mermaids. The Punta San Francesco peninsula shelters the northern part of the beach from the mistral winds.

THE BAY OF PIZZOMUNNO

What gives this bay its name is a large 25-meter-high monolith called Pizzomunno, about which a sad legend hovers:

> ❝In fact, the legend tells of a young boy named Pizzomunno, who was in love with the young Cristalda. Every night, when he was out at sea fishing, Pizzomunno was tempted by the sirens' calls, calls to which the young fisherman yielded. Then the sirens, jealous of Cristalda, decided to kidnap her and take her to the depths of the sea. The boy, from his pain, turned into the huge white rock that can be seen today. Thus it was that the sirens, moved to compassion, allowed the two lovers to be able to meet again once every 100 years.❞

The beach is considered one of the most beautiful of all the Gargano: as mentioned earlier, it has lovely golden sand and crystal-clear waters and is lapped by a cliff.

It features numerous services and is also within walking distance, given its proximity to the town.

Fun fact: tradition says that whoever makes a complete circle around the Pizzomunno monolith will be able to fulfill one's wish.

SCIALMARINO BEACH

Scialmarino Beach is located in Vieste, within the Gargano National Park, in a natural area that also includes a forest, lakes, and picturesque villages. The beach is 3 km long, and its crystal-clear waters are warmer than most of Vieste's coastline. The seabed is exceptionally shallow, which makes bathing safe for children. Because it is exposed to winds from the north and northeast, the beach is popular with surfers, kite-surfers and windsurfers. The beach is free, but nearby bathing establishments still offer facilities for an enjoyable day at the beach. From the beach, you can also see the Porticello trebuchet. The Trabucco is a wooden structure used in the past for fishing, is included in the cultural heritage of the Gargano. Several can be found along the coast, many of which have been restored

CHIANCA BEACH

Chianca beach is located 8 km north of Vieste and is named after the rock in the bay's center. The beach is about 200 meters wide and has a shallow sandy seabed, suitable for both those with children and those who like to dive. A striking feature of the area is a sea cave partially open at the top, which was once a refuge for some monk seals.

CROVATICO BEACH

Crovatico Beach is a little-known beach located in a hidden bay along the north coast of Vieste, about 10 km from the town center. It is protected by thick vegetation and the cliff that surrounds it. There is no road to reach it since it is surrounded by a holiday village that occupies the entire inland side. Access is possible only through the town, or the cliff, in case you want to climb it. The beach is very quiet and relaxing because of this not-so-easy access. The sandy beach has crystal clear waters and shallow, gently sloping seabed. Located north of the Gargano, it is exposed to the Mistral and Tramontana winds and sheltered from winds coming from the south, such as the sirocco and libeccio. The presence of the reef, however, makes the area not particularly windswept.

PESCHICI AND THE BAY OF MANACCORA

Vieste is surrounded by beautiful beaches known for their natural beauty. But it is not the only one: proceeding north, particularly following the road to the town of Peschici, it is possible to reach the wonderful Manaccora Bay: Manaccora Beach is famous for the extraordinary beauty of its nature and its crystal-clear waters. During the summer season, it exerts a strong tourist attraction, thanks also to a wide range of water activities such as snorkeling or being able to dive, while equally high is the offer of the various accommodations and restaurants in the surroundings.

Manaccora is also known for the "trabucchi," these ancient fishing structures typical of the Gargano region. Trabucchi are built on stilts, allowing them to extend to sea and make it easier for fishermen to use their nets in deep water.

Manaccora's Trabucchi is particularly famous for their beauty and panoramic location, allowing spectacular coastline and beach views. Today the trabucchi are used as restaurants or for tourist activities, which allows for unique and crazy views of the Gargano coastline while sampling the local cuisine.

TREMITI ISLANDS ARCHIPELAGO

The Tremiti Islands are an Italian archipelago located in the Adriatic Sea, 12 miles off the coast of Gargano. Their power of attraction is due to the clarity of the waters and the pristine, clean seabed. The climate is pleasant for much of the year, while the air proves unpolluted, the vegetation lush, with unspoiled wilderness. The coastline features bays, headlands, low and sandy shores, and high and rocky cliffs with sheer cliffs.

The archipelago comprises five islands: San Domino, San Nicola, Capraia, Cretaccio, and Pianosa. San Domino is the largest island covered with an Aleppo pine forest, while San Nicola is rich in historical and artistic monuments. Capraia, on the other hand, is covered with grasses and flowers. Cretaccio is the smallest of the islands, the largest rock in the entire archipelago, while Pianosa is part of the Marine Park reserve. All the islands have small inlets and coves, some well-known, such as Cala delle Arene, Cala Matano, and Cala degli Inglesi.

The Tremiti Islands were once known as "Insulae Diomedeae," named after the Greek hero Diomedes, whose burial place was believed to be in the archipelago.

Legend has it that Diomedes, after the Trojan War, discovering the conspiracy hatched against him by his wife and her lover, fled and took refuge on the coast of Gargano, where he married the daughter of King Dauno, here he threw three boulders into the sea that gave rise to the islands of San Domino, San Nicola, and Capraia.

Legend also says that Diomedes died during a duel and that his fellow adventurers, transformed into birds by the goddess Venus, wept and watched over his grave. ❧

The documented history of the Tremiti begins with the construction of the Santa Maria a Mare abbey on the island of San Nicola, which was expanded by the Benedictines and fortified by Charles II of Anjou. Then, in the 19th century, King Ferdinand II of the Two Sicilies settled several destitute people from the Neapolitan slums to repopulate the islands, who were thus able to take advantage of the sea's abundance of fish, giving rise to a second colonization of the Tremiti.

THE SEA PARK

The Tremiti Islands Marine Park, established in 1989 and included in the Garga-no National Park, is one of the most beautiful natural habitats in the Mediterra-nean, a nature reserve encompassing the coastal area surrounding the five is-lands with a unique fish stock of fish and crustaceans that live protected in the depths of the sea. The underwater panorama of the Tremiti is of rare beauty. Scuba diving allows visitors to appreciate the natural treasure and the many relics and shipwrecks. The economy of the Tremiti Islands is based mainly on fishing and summer tourism. However, the wild nature and rugged coastline have encouraged slow tourism, making it an ideal destination for those seeking a vacation in total freedom in contact with nature. Nowhere else offers the same warm, genuine, and relaxing atmosphere as the Tremiti Islands.

LAKES OF LESINA AND VARANO

Another Gargano area of unspoiled natural beauty is the two lakes of Lesina and Varano, located in the northernmost part of the Gargano area. Their proximity to the Adriatic Sea means that the water in both lakes is salty.

As with the Tremiti Islands, tourism in this area is designed for those who want to get in touch with nature, perhaps observing the countless species of birds that make this area a place to nest or winter. The fish fauna also features fascinating species.

This is why there are several laws and restrictions in place to protect the area, and anyone visiting both lakes is required to observe and respect them.

Several portions of both lakes are considered protected areas. Mass tourism would be detrimental to the ecosystem of these delicate environments, which they are trying to preserve.

There are several activities that can be carried out at the lakes of Lesina and Varano: near the natural area of Lake Lesina is the visitor center "Laguna di Lesina," from which it is possible to organize guided excursions both on foot on land and by the sea with boats such as sandals and catamarans. Night fishing and sport fishing are also possible, as well as birdwatching.

LAKE LESINA

Lake Lesina covers about 50 square kilometers. It is the shallowest, whose bottom fluctuates between 70 centimeters and 2 meters deep. A strip of land separates the lake from the Adriatic Sea, with which it communicates through the two channels Acquarotta and Schiaparo.

The eastern part of the lake is considered a protected area. Here, fish and migratory birds have found an ideal habitat to thrive and nest. In addition, Lake Lesina is navigable, and several companies offer this service.

Sailing the lake at sunset can be a unique experience, as can walking along the shores of the lake. Here the setting of the sun creates an incredible spectacle.

In Lesina, there is a 400-meter-long footbridge that allows you to walk along the lake until you reach the remains of an islet dedicated to St. Clement, now used by birds for nesting, on which a monastery once stood.

Near Lesina, it is possible to see fishermen whose techniques are still those used by their ancestors. Here, in fact, eel fishing is a significant tradition.

LAKE OF VARANO

Lake Varano, the largest lake in Italy, is separated from the sea by a strip of beach (considered a protected area) and has an area of 60 square kilometers, and within it, there is also an island, considered a protected area, home to many species of birds and plants.

Boat trips and fishing can also be organized here.

A tip for those who love to ride a bike: there is a dedicated bike path called "Pista Ciclabile del Lago di Varano. It is a path that winds along the coast of Lake Varano, about 20km long, offering incredible panoramic views of the body of water and the surrounding hills. The route is suitable for everyone, as it is flat and has no particular technical difficulties.

The bike route runs between the town of Vieste and the Varano Nature Reserve. It passes through many towns and villages, such as Mattinata, Peschici, and Vico del Gargano. It is an excellent opportunity to admire the extraordinary beauty of

this stretch of Gargano coastline while also stopping in the various villages and enjoying what they offer.

Lake Varano is navigable. In fact, several companies offer this service, providing different types of boats.

A unique experience for those who love nature and adventure could be to visit the lake by kayak. The lake is ideal for kayaking, from which, while paddling, you can admire the lush vegetation and rich wildlife, including waterfowl and fish. By kayak, you can navigate between the lake's islands, where you can reach caves and different inlets. While sailing, it is also possible to spot dolphins and sea turtles. To visit the lake by kayak, it is advisable to do so with an experienced guide or in an organized group. Several on-site companies provide kayak rental services and logistical support for organized excursions.

The undoubtedly most evocative area of Lake Varano is its eastern part: in fact, here it is possible to see a wooden statue from the 1300s depicting Jesus Christ, placed in the middle of the lake, about which various legends hover.

One such legend states that the one depicted is the true face of Christ and that the statue itself is a reminder of the cross that was on top of the church of a nearby village, obliterated by the wrath of God because of the impiety of its inhabitants.

The lake area is full of caves. The most famous of these caves is that of St. Michael the Archangel (in this area, religious tourism is very strong, later, we will talk about two other important shrines also in the same area, one of which is related to the same archangel).

Legend says that St. Michael the Archangel had escaped from the nearby town of St. Mark and hid in one of the many cavities in the area and, to leave a sign of his passage, imprinted the shape of his wings on the rock. ❧

The cave's interior contains all the natural elements typical of the environment: stalactites and stalagmites, rocks, and a basin containing water with miraculous powers. The bay is named "Pila di Santa Lucia," a saint traditionally considered the patron saint of sight, so much so that tourists stop to wet their fingers to rub them over their eyes. At the entrance to the cave, it is possible to see what legend says are the imprint of the saint's wings and his horse's hoof.

Unfortunately, dampness has almost completely obliterated the frescoes, while graffiti and inscriptions left by visitors over the centuries can be seen on the floor.

This mixture of religion, history, and legend is found almost everywhere in Italy, but it is particularly pronounced in this area.

Two other religious places annually attract thousands, if not millions, of faithful and non-faithful people from all over the world: we are talking about San Giovanni Rotondo, the place where Padre Pio lived, and the sanctuary of St. Michael the Archangel.

A RELIGIOUS TOURISM: SAN GIOVANNI ROTONDO AND MONTE SANT'ANGELO

The town of San Giovanni Rotondo is famous for housing the remains of Padre Pio, a monk of the Capuchin order who, according to Christian tradition, bore the marks of Christ's passion on his body for many years. Millions of pilgrims come each year to pay homage to the saint's remains.

The presence of this figure for long years has made the small Gargano town a true center of religious tourism, where it is possible to visit:

1. The church of Santa Maria delle Grazie, where are the saint's remains, the golden altar, and the moonstone with the trace of the stigmata;
2. The new church of St. Pio, built in 2003;
3. The monastery caves where the friar prayed;
4. The civic museum dedicated to Padre Pio.

Much of San Giovanni Rotondo's tourism revolves around this figure, considered sacred. However, remember that we are in the heart of the Gargano, and its national park with the Umbra Forest, which we will discuss later.

If the cult of Padre Pio is pretty recent, since his life took place in the last century, the cult that grew up for the Archangel Michael in Monte Sant'Angelo is much older.

The same saint we have already encountered at Lake Varano appears to have also appeared here.

Legend has it that a local man had lost a bull and found it inside a cave. Seized with fury, he kills the bull by shooting an arrow at it. However, the arrow changes its path, thunders back, and wounds the man.

After the news of the prodigious event spread and ecclesiastical representatives were called to verify what had happened, the Archangel appeared, explaining that he had diverted the course of the arrow.

The second apparition was on the occasion of a siege by the Goths on the city of Siponto; here, St. Michael appeared to the bishop to say that everything would soon end with a victory for the local population and the retreat of the Goths.

The cave of the first apparition was elevated to a shrine that became a destination for pilgrims, but especially for crusaders, who, before leaving for the Holy Land, passed by Mount St. Michael as a sign of devotion and to ask to be protected from the dangers of the journey to the Holy Land.

Ideally, this very ancient shrine, known since the 6th century, is linked to other important shrines scattered throughout Europe:

- St Michael's Mount (Cornwall);
- Mont Saint Michel (France);
- Sacra di San Michele in the Susa Valley;
- The Hermitage of San Michele di Coli near Bobbio.

Monte Sant'Angelo is considered a UNESCO heritage site precisely because of the shrine and the traces left here by the Lombard population.

The town's historic center is also considered heritage to be protected: walking through the narrow medieval streets, you get the impression that time has stood still centuries ago. It should be considered that the town stands on a point that towers over the entire Gargano, which contributes to a truly unique and evocative atmosphere.

Among these narrow streets, it is possible to catch a glimpse of the skill of the local artisans, who, thanks to their ability to work with wood, stone, and wrought iron, create objects dedicated to religious worship as well as utensils for daily life.

In the upper part of the town also stands the castle, which dominates the area below, dating from the Middle Ages and built by the Normans. The castle today houses a museum with historical artifacts dating back to the Middle Ages and the Renaissance.

A legend associated with the castle has it that the ghost of Bianca Lancia, fourth wife of Emperor Frederick of Swabia, roams its rooms; out of jealousy, he kept her segregated in the castle. Finally, the woman, tired of this confinement, decided to throw herself off the castle's highest tower. From that moment on, her ghost wanders the rooms of the structure with cries and cries, dressed in a light white dress.

This wonderful village, precisely because of its history and culture, can be considered an actual open-air museum: among the various monuments to visit, we also have the monumental complex of San Pietro, which encloses the baptistery of San Giovanni and the church of Santa Maria Maggiore.

The territory of Monte Sant'Angelo also includes another element that has been named a UNESCO heritage site, this time of natural origin: the beech forests of Monte Sant'Angelo.

This forested area is of great ecological importance, home to a beech forest over 500 years old. The beech forests are an ideal habitat for several species of birds and insects and an important wildlife refuge. Various hikes and nature walks can be taken in the area, admiring the beauty of the local vegetation and wildlife. The beech forests of Monte Sant'Angelo are also a place of great historical and cultural value, as they have been used as hunting grounds since ancient times.

These beech forests are located within the magnificent Umbra Forest, which we will discuss below.

THE UMBRIAN FOREST AND ITS MAGNIFICENCE

The Umbra Forest is an important part of Gargano Park, covering 10,000 hectares and having areas that reach up to 800 meters above sea level and almost touching the sea.

The Umbra Forest is so called because of the dense vegetation whereby the sun's rays can hardly get through the barrier created by the plants.

It is an area considered most important for several reasons:

- There is 40% of the Italian flora; 70% of the birds nesting in Italy;
- It is possible to study the phenomenon of macrosomatism: plants are larger than the norm;
- There are more than 2000 plant species: beeches, oaks, holm, downy oaks, maples, Aleppo pines, and many others as one descends towards the sea, where the vegetation takes on more of the typical characteristics of the Mediterranean maquis; The fauna is very rich and varied: roe deer, badgers, dormice, eagle owls, barn owls, to name just a few.

There are several areas designed for children, such as an artificial lake where they can observe and feed carp, catfish, toads, and other aquatic animals.

There is also an area where there are deer, with whom you can interact, thanks to the presence of a net.

Still, near this area, a magnificent playground is designed for the youngest children.

For the older ones, several and numerous trails can be followed, both on foot and by bike.

The Umbrian Forest is a truly enchanting place where you can touch the purest and wildest nature and breathe uncontaminated air.

My only advice: always bring something warm to wear, even in the middle of summer. As mentioned, the sun's rays hardly reach the ground, making the forest have a totally different climate than outside it.

FOODS TO ABSOLUTELY ENJOY IN THE GARGANO AREA

There are several gastronomic specialties in the Gargano. Here the sea's flavors meet the hinterland›s flavors, resulting in dishes characterized by strong flavors using simple ingredients.

These dishes, in addition to enhancing the products of the area, bear witness to a thousand-year-old culinary tradition.

Here is what you absolutely must taste:

The fish soup, called "ciambott" by the locals, made with very fresh and delicious fish;

The caciocavallo, a typical Apulian cheese, here produced in its podolica variant: the milk used comes from podolica cows raised in the semi-wild state. After aging, caciocavallo is a feast for the palate.

Paposcia, a sandwich stuffed with cheese and grilled vegetables, all produced locally;

At Lake Lesina, I recommend tasting eel, prepared in various ways, and a prized wild herb, salicornia, also known as sea asparagus.

The Gargano is also famous for citrus production, especially fragrant oranges, and lemons.

As for the wines, these are those typical of the Gargano area.

Nero di Troia: highly prized black wine, the production of which has also enabled some economic growth in the area. It has a very dark color and a characteristically spicy flavor. While in the past it tended to be mixed with other "gentler" wines given its qualities, for the past few years it has begun to be produced to keep it pure, with excellent characteristics.

Cacc'e Mitt: wine suitable for accompanying first courses, especially ragú sauce, with an intense aroma and a full, harmonious flavor. Its name derives from the fact that those who possessed the tools for crushing grapes made them available to different vintners who, by the end of the day, had to complete all the operations to allow another vintner to crush them.

San Severo: wine with three variants, red, rosé and white. It is particularly suitable for enjoying with typical Gargano products such as fish and seafood.

CHAPTER 2

APULIA AND THE SEA: BARI AND THE ADRIATIC CITIES

Moving down south, we come to the heart of Puglia: focusing on the side that faces the Adriatic, there are lovely towns full of history, traditions, great food, and more.

A series of sandy and rocky beaches, dunes, cliffs, sea caves, and a wide range of wildlife and flora characterize the coast. The Apulian Adriatic coast is highly popular for summer tourism, thanks to a beautiful sea, unparalleled scenic beauty, delicious cuisine like few in the world, and cities that can welcome tourists but not only, also full of historical treasures to discover and visit. In short, the Apulian Adriatic coast is one of the most popular tourist destinations in the region, with a long tradition of tourism, great cultural and recreational offerings, warm hospitality, and many services to suit every need.

BARI

Let's start immediately with what is the largest city in Puglia, as well as the region's capital, the magnificent city of Bari.

I am particularly attached to this city because it is only half an hour from the small town where I was born, raised, and currently live, so I have had several opportunities to experience the beauty that Bari has to offer fully.

Bari will overwhelm you with its enthusiasm, traditions, food, and beauty.

A saying goes like this: "If Paris had the sea, it would be a little Bari."

The cheerfulness of the people of Bari is irrepressible; they will welcome you like family members, ready to guide you through the city's beauty and make you feel at home. They will immediately offer you what are typical foods, among the best in the world:

- Panzerotti
- Orecchiette con le cime di rape
- Crudo di mare
- Fresh homemade pasta with meat sauce

CATHEDRAL OF SAINT NICOLAS

Among the first places you should visit is the basilica of St. Nicholas: the protector of the city.

The church is an example of Apulian Romanesque, where Norman and Byzantine elements are blended. It was erected in the 11th century on the ruins of an earlier Byzantine church, which arose on the ruins of a pagan temple. The church consists of three large naves with a chancel and a semicircular apse. The crypt below contains part of the relics of St. Nicholas, whose body was stolen from Myra, Turkey, by some Italian merchants in 1087. it is also possible to observe magnificent frescoes dating from the 12th century.

The church is the site of a pilgrimage from all parts of the world, the figure of St. Nicholas being the object of worship and devotion by different religious denominations.

During the patronal feast days in May, the Bari waterfront fills with people, lights, sounds, and music. The festive air is everywhere, so great is the devotion of the entire city to the patron saint. Civil and religious events create a unique atmosphere to be experienced firsthand.

BASILICA OF SAN SABINO

Walking through the narrow streets of Bari's old town, not far from the cathedral, is another Apulian Romanesque-style church dating from the same period as the basilica: the Cathedral of St. Sabinus, inside whose crypt are the remains of the saint.

The cathedral's facade is of white stone decorated with geometric patterns, animals, and a rose window, while inside, there are Byzantine mosaics on the floor.

NORMAN-SWABIAN CASTLE

As well as the cathedral, the castle overlooks the sea and is located in the old part of the city.

Built in the 12th century by the Normans, the Swabians later expanded it. Today it houses a medieval museum that is well worth seeing. From the well-preserved central tower, it is possible to see an overview of the entire city and its beautiful sea.

For information, you can visit the official Facebook page or the website:

https://musei.puglia.beniculturali.it/musei/castello-svevo- di-bari/

Staying still in the old town, getting lost in the alleys and lanes can lead you to discover priceless treasures: unique views, breathtaking views, but also crafts and traditions that, despite efforts to protect, are disappearing.

One of the most famous streets in old Bari is the so-called "Strada delle orecchiette": here, you will find old women intent on making fresh pasta typical of the place, ready to welcome you with their enthusiasm and cheerfulness, and from whom you can also buy the pasta they make every day. Not only that, if you want you can book a lunch or dinner prepared by these women, of course, based on orecchiette!

ST NICHOLAS PIER

On the other hand, if you want to taste raw fish such as sea urchins or octopus, accompanied by a bottle of strictly "Peroni" beer, St. Nicholas Pier is the best place. Here you can see fishermen's spears loaded with freshly caught fish ready to be sold. In addition, if you are lucky, you will be able to witness a "ritual" handed down from fisherman to fisherman over the centuries: the curling of the octopus. A process that is divided into several stages and is designed to make the octopus more tender. Not suitable for the faint-hearted, it nevertheless remains a truly unique process.

From the San Nicola pier, you can see the Margherita Theater and walk along Bari's magnificent waterfront.

The historic center of Bari is wonderful, and I will never tire of saying that. Besides gorgeous places, here you can taste the best of the best that Bari cuisine offers.

The city is teeming with places where you can taste incredible delicacies, including focaccia, panzerotti, rice potatoes and mussels, orecchiette with sauce, and braciole.

We'll point you to a few places, but we assure you that there are more than a few places where you can taste great food. If you want to taste focaccia made according to tradition, then the right place is the "Panificio Fiore," located behind the cathedral in "Strada palazzo di Città, 38."

As for panzerotti, you can usually also find them where focaccia is sold. However, we recommend "Cibò" in Piazza Mercantile, where you can enjoy several variations of them, open, however, only from 8:30 p.m. onward. You can choose from a wide variety of fillings for panzerotti. Still, the one that most represents Bari is the panzerotto stuffed with minced meat and turnip tops, vegetables that grow flavorfully and luxuriantly in the Murgia area and that you won't be able to taste anywhere else.

If, on the other hand, you are undecided and don't really know your way around, several agencies offer different packages of historical-gastronomic tours through the streets of old Bari, where alongside the secrets of history that lurk in the alleyways, you can savor the best of the best in local cuisine.

Bari food tours:

https://www.civitatis.com/it/bari/tour-gastronomico-bari/?aid= 6811&cmp=vederebari

Walking tours and homemade pasta:

https://www.getyourguide.it/bari-l721/bari-tour-a-piedi-e-pasta- fatta-in-casa-t181841/?partner_id=XE5R8WQ&utm_medium= platforms_and_communities&placement=button-cta&cmp= vederebari&deeplink_id=38a147ae-c226-5bfa-9e1f-1258086650c8

Guided tour of Bari:

https://www.civitatis.com/it/bari/visita-guidata-bari/?aid= 6811&cmp=vederebari

Guided tours and street food:

https://www.getyourguide.it/bari-l721/bari-tour-a-piedi-con-cibo-di- strada-t181481/?partner_id=XE5R8WQ&utm_medium= platforms_and_communities&placement=button-cta&cmp= vederebari&deeplink_id=83b09fcc-d40d-5664-a14d-c0d7092051db

TRANI, THE PEARL OF THE ADRIATIC

Another wonderful city overlooking the Adriatic, the city of Trani is located further north than Bari, and is a true wonder to discover and visit.

Precisely because of its beauty and the treasures it contains, Trani is considered a "city of art," so much so that it has earned the nickname "Pearl of the Adriatic."

TRANI CATHEDRAL

When one speaks of Trani, the thought immediately runs to its magnificent cathedral that rises above the sea and dominates the large square in front, combining its white color with the colors of the sea and sky, creating a fascinating contrast.

In fact, the structure, dedicated to St. Nicholas Pellegrino and erected in the 12th century, was built using a stone typical of these places, white tuff.

Inside we find mosaics and works of art of great value. In general, the church is considered a splendid example of the Gothic architecture of southern Italy.

The church can be visited free of charge, while a ticket is charged to climb the bell tower.

THE HARBOR OF TRANI

Another symbolic place of the city is its harbor, from which not only goods and people pass and have passed, but also centuries of history.

Built on an inlet, it is always bustling with life and movement, full of fine establishments ready to send your taste buds into a feast, but also ideal for an evening stroll amid the moon reflecting in the water and boats being rocked by the gentle movement of the waves.

The port is also one of the landing points for cruises passing through the Adriatic.

HISTORIC CENTER

The historic center of Trani looks like a maze of narrow streets and small squares, with houses and buildings made of white stone, in which the smells coming out of the many restaurants present permeate. I recommend stopping, even if only to enjoy a coffee or ice cream, while enjoying the quiet and serenity atmosphere of one of Puglia's most beautiful towns.

Within the historic center, it is worth visiting the church of All Saints and the Jewish quarter with the synagogue.

SWABIAN CASTLE

Another place rich in history and charm is the Swabian-Norman castle, a fine example of Apulian medieval architecture.

The castle stands on a rocky promontory above the sea and, like Bari's, is of Norman origin, with extensions in later centuries.

The castle is perfectly visitable in all its structures, it also houses a museum with various artifacts, and it is something not to be missed.

But how is it possible that we are talking about one of the most beautiful coastlines and we have not yet mentioned its beaches?

BEACHES IN TRANI

Trani's beaches are characterized by alternating stretches of fine, golden sand with others composed of pebbles. The water is always crystal clear.

The strong presence of services and accommodation facilities means that every tourist or visitor can satisfy their needs, whether they want to relax or go searching for adventure.

Facilities on the Cristoforo Colombo promenade, as well as those on the Mongelli promenade, provide a wide range of services to please both families with children and the grim of young people looking for fun.

BARLETTA AND MOLFETTA

Let's stay still north of Bari to meet two more splendid cities on the Adriatic coast, two charming towns full of life, in which ancient and modern merge, creating a scenario that cannot help but surprise those who visit them. We are talking about Barletta and Molfetta.

BARLETTA

Barletta is also considered a city of art, with a port that has always been a very important landing and departure point over the centuries.

The first thing that comes to mind when thinking of Barletta is the famous "disfida": in 1503, thirteen Italian knights (who sided with the Spanish), and 13 French knights, fought over a matter of honor as part of the struggle for control of the territory. Victory went to the Italians, led by Ettore Fieramosca, an Italian leader.

Such "disfida" is annually commemorated with a giant re-enactment of those events, involving the entire city with processions, performances, figures, and events related to the entire historical context of the city in the 1500s. Typically such a major event takes place between late August and October.

The re-enactment is engaging and exciting, as the whole city seems to return 500 years ago. The spectacle and atmosphere that is created is truly amazing and incredible.

WHAT TO SEE IN BARLETTA

Like other Adriatic cities, Barletta is not only sea, but also history, art, and culture.

For example, its Norman-era castle houses a library, the Barletta Civic Museum, which includes artifacts and artifacts related to the city's history, as well as paintings by great past artists and a lapidarium, a collection of stone inscriptions and funerary monuments in Greek and Latin. The history of a region inhabited since ancient times emerges through tombstones, epigraphs and other artifacts. The "De Nittis" picture gallery is also worth visiting, dedicated precisely to the impressionist painter from Barletta (also known by the much better-known French impressionist painters). The picture gallery was once housed in the castle; however, it was feared that the proximity to the sea might damage the canvases, and it was preferred to move it to the Marra palace.

For art lovers and non-art lovers alike, it is worth seeing, especially for the organized temporary exhibitions.

BASILICA OF THE HOLY SEPULCHRE

The Basilica of the Holy Sepulcher is one of those places you absolutely must visit.

Apparently, it was founded by the Knights of the Holy Sepulcher returning from the holy land, and today it houses several treasures, some of them directly from Palestine. Numerous frescoes can be seen.

The other wonder next to the basilica is the "Colossus of Barletta," considered one of the greatest examples of Byzantine sculpture. The bronze statue, 4.50 m high, would represent the Byzantine emperor Theodosius II.

If you want to enjoy Barletta's beaches and sea, there is a seafront promenade fully equipped with services and eateries. In contrast, the two beaches of Ponente and Levante are easily accessible and ideal as much for relaxing as for those looking for fun.

THE INNER PART

When we talked about Barletta as a city of history and culture, reference was also made to the hinterland: first of all, the magnificent Castel del Monte, which we will talk about later, and then the archaeological park of Canne della Battaglia, where the clash between Rome and Carthage led by the leader Hannibal took place. Visiting this area means retracing the region's entire history, from prehistory to the Middle Ages. In fact, there are numerous finds, fragments, and ruins that testify to the extent to which humans have always inhabited these places.

Visiting the hinterland of Barletta also means seeing what the extreme edges of the Murgia area, within which other inestimable natural and historical beauties are waiting to be discovered by travelers are.

MOLFETTA

The other Adriatic town north of Bari that we want to talk about is Molfetta, located between Bari and Barletta, a quiet and welcoming seaside town where you can enjoy the beach to relax, do activities, or even go in search of its extraordinary cultural, gastronomic, and natural treasures.

Let's start with the sea: the waters here are crystal clear and limpid, with a predominantly rocky coastline.

There are few free beaches, especially those near the city, where private lidos take care to meet any kind of special need or condition. The sea in Molfetta is also well-known because anyone can easily access it.

Notable among the free beaches is Cala San Giacomo, a very old city port that later fell into disuse. The view is wonderful, and here nature has decided to combine sand, pebbles, and rocks. Even sitting and watching the scenery in a quiet area can prove to be something fulfilling, from which to spiritually get in touch with the soul of this beautiful sea and its equally wonderful nature. In addition, you can bring your animal friends for much of the area of this ancient harbor. What could be better than enjoying a beautiful landscape with your four-legged friend?

The other free beach is Prima Cala, where a small pine forest surrounds a mixture of pebbles and sand. This, as well as Cala Sant'Andrea, has some facilities to allow disabled people to swim.

Molfettesi's free beaches are often considered by those who love tranquility and seek proper relaxation.

If, on the other hand, the intention is to try one's hand at doing activities, whatever they may be, or to always have comfort at hand, there are many private lidos available such as Lido Bahia or Villaggio Lido Nettuno, which both day and night are always active and with many proposals made available to vacationers.

HISTORIC CENTER

Like many other villages in the surrounding area, Molfetta has centuries of history and art behind it. And here, too, the historic center, which stands on a small promontory called " St. Andrew's Island" with its peculiar herringbone structure, awaits you with its scents and flavors to make you relive the atmosphere of the past, in its narrow, winding streets, among which we find ancient churches and palaces set.

On the edge of the historic center stands the cathedral of St. Conrad, located by the sea and artistically distinctive, considered a splendid example of unique Apulian Romanesque architecture.

In fact, the nave has a singular feature: three aligned domes of different sizes along the entire length of the center. The arrangement of the chianche roofing is very reminiscent of the trulli of Alberobello, while the exterior features twin bell towers 39 meters high. A place that certainly does not go unnoticed.

The historic center is charming: among a café, restaurants and many churches with a few secrets hidden inside, such as the Baroque church of San Pietro with its tower towering over the entire old town.

Staying in the historic center, we find the Passari tower: a circular structure on 3 floors built in the 1500s for defensive purposes. Today, however, it hosts exhibitions and cultural events, while from its top, you can enjoy a fabulous view of the city and the Adriatic Sea.

Next to the cathedral is the splendid port, a wonderful place that houses a large lighthouse and a series of shipyards, which can be visited with a guide: they are some of the last remaining in Apulia and have been active since the Middle Ages.

BEYOND THE CITY

Outside the town is a special church, the Church of Our Lady of the Martyrs, built in the Middle Ages next to a shelter where knights returning from the Crusades were treated. Together with St. Conrad, this saintly figure is the town's patron saint, and every year her statue is carried in procession by the sea.

THE PULO OF MOLFETTA

We remain outside the city, and this time we talk about a truly unique place: the Pulo of Molfetta.

The Pulo is nothing but a doline, a cavity due to the erosive action of water on limestone rock.

The one in Molfetta has a diameter of 170 m for a maximum depth of 30 m. Caves and natural cavities are present along the walls.

The Pulo has its importance both in terms of biodiversity and because important finds, some of which date back to the Neolithic period, have been found.

The Pulo can be visited free of charge, although reservations are required.

There is also a civic museum dedicated to the Pulo, which contains a variety of artifacts from the Neolithic to the 1800s, a period when it was exploited to extract mineral products.

If you still want to explore the coast north of Bari, the advice is to pass through the two towns of Giovinazzo and Bisceglie. In these places, too, culture and tradition go hand in hand with the search for fun and carefree living.

POLIGNANO AND MONOPOLI

This time we move further south than Bari to discover two other seaside towns that are more than wonderful, and amazing and have been experiencing incredible development in recent years: Monopoli and Polignano a Mare.

All of these towns on the Adriatic are experiencing a very strong development, with the number of tourists increasing yearly, and consequently, the supply is also adjusting to the demand.

Let's start with Monopoli: the first thing that stands out about Monopoli is the huge historic center, called the "old town" by the locals.

Initially, you may be overwhelmed by its size, but soon you become fascinated by the ancient squares, noble palaces, and whitewashed houses. In addition, this area has a high concentration of cultural heritage and churches.

Walking through the narrow-cobbled streets and arches, you can smell the sea air and scents of local food. At nightfall, the fishing fleet arrives at the harbor, and a veritable microcosm comes alive with sounds, scents, and colors representing the values of Mediterranean and Levantine traditions. Within the old town are numerous restaurants and trattorias where you can enjoy excellent fresh fish. There are also bars and clubs for young people, as well as artisans' stores and grocery stores. In this historic area, everything is at your fingertips.

16TH CENTURY CASTLE

An important element of the historic center is the 16th-century castle built by Charles V, part of the defensive system of fortifications desired by the emperor.

The castle's perimeter is characterized by five pentagonal bastions, while much of the ancient walls are still excellently preserved.

Inside the castle, there are very interesting spaces to visit:

- A 10th-century rock church dedicated to St. Nicholas;
- The weapons room, with four gunboats at "water's edge," two facing the sea, the other two facing the harbor;
- A large Roman gate with two guardhouses and two octagonal towers incorporated into the castle's structure: the latter was erected on ancient Messapian walls, based on a fortification that is traced back to prehistoric times.

THE SEA OF MONOPOLI

Monopoli is also famous for its crystal-clear water sea and splendid 15 km of beach. In fact, there are several awards from different bodies for the beauty and quality of the sea waters that bathe this magnificent seaside town.

In addition, the beaches of Monopoli are distinguished to the north and toward the center by the succession of low cliffs to inlets and coves, while to the south, there are long stretches of sand.

A landscape that, thanks to the many services and facilities present, allows for various activities, such as surfing, boat trips or exploration.

It is also possible to visit the cliffs, that is, caves created by the erosive action of the waters on the rock. If you are brave enough, there are some cold currents along the coast where you can dive.

I suggest some of the beaches in Monopoli that you absolutely must see:

CALA PORTA VECCHIA

This beach is one of the most famous in Monopoli. It has shallow waters and is easily accessible. If you are fond of photography, this beach hosts between September and November the "PhEst," an international festival of photography and more, which involves the whole town with exhibitions and events.

Porto Rosso

Porto Rosso beach is very popular due to its advantageous location and size. It consists of fine sand with a shallow seabed and crystal-clear water, making it ideal for families with young children and young people. During the summer, concerts are often organized here.

Porto Bianco

The conformation of this cove, with wide beach and shallow water, is among the favorites for those with children. Ramps and wooden stairs facilitate its access.

It is also considered the ideal starting point to reach nearby beaches by boat.

Cala Paradiso

This bay, entirely surrounded by cliffs, can be easily reached by public transportation.

The area is in private hands who organize different kinds of sports activities and events. There are also summer camps here organized by neighboring countries.

Porto Paradiso

Despite its centrality to the town, this small sandy beach is favored by those seeking tranquility and convenience, thanks to the services provided by private individuals. It is easily reached by public transportation.

Porto Marzano

This small beach is also sandy, and to reach it you have to walk along a path surrounded by greenery.

Because of the rock walls surrounding it, and the rocky outcrop near the shore, this beach is also known as "Devil's Peak."

Cala Sott ile

Like the previous beach, this bay is hidden and can be reached by a dirt path that runs alongside a campsite.

Thanks to the pine forest surrounding the small bay, the waters remain calm and peaceful even on the windiest days.

RUPESTRIAN CIVILIZATION

Traces of an ancient past can be found in every corner of Apulia. Monopoli is no exception in this. You can treat yourself to a magnificent experience with a hike among Byzantine frescoes, rare rock churches and houses carved into the rock.

These places are lost or hidden in the historic center and make for an exciting hike, making you feel like you are the protagonist of an adventure movie. The rock churches are evidence of ancient worship that survived the barbarian hordes and Saracen assaults. They were carved into the rock and entirely frescoed. The greatest presence of these rock settlements is recorded south of the city. The territory lends itself very well to developing a rock civilization due to the presence of "lame," small canyons of karst origin that slope down toward the sea.

Visiting these settlements takes on a special charm, as it means moving in search of art treasures and early forms of Christianity in this area. These houses and churches were created as "negative architecture" by digging into the rock,

out of sight of possible enemies, during an age when assaults, especially from the sea, were frequent. First to inhabit these "shelters" were the Greek-Apulian monks who followed the rule of St. Basil. These churches were the meeting point between East and West, between Catholic liturgy and Greek Orthodox worship, which overlapped and merged into a single mindset and religious expression. Some of these churches existed as early as 1180, as confirmed by a bull of Pope Alexander III.

PHEST

Monopoli has been hosting The PhEst, an open-air exhibition of photography and art of international caliber for the past few years. It aims to investigate the relationship between the Mediterranean Sea and those who overlook its basin.

So not only Monopoli and Apulia but also the Balkan areas, North Africa, and the Middle East are involved in this splendid series of events in which the whole city participates, and the best photographers from around the world beyond leave their mark. The festival takes place between September and November through events, stages, and routes.

POLIGNANO A MARE

We now come to one of the most beautiful places in the region: Polignano a Mare.

Polignano is simply gorgeous, and this is evidenced by the fact that the number of registered tourists increases dramatically year by year.

Anyone who has been to Polignano a Mare can only speak of it in one way: positively.

The first thing that steals the spirit of those who arrive in town is a beautiful deep blue sea, whose waves go poetically crashing over cliffs and sea caves, many of which can be visited.

But Polignano's beauty does not end there: its historic center, built on a rocky outcrop, spreads out among white hovels and Baroque-era buildings that, starting from the marquis arch, wind through a maze of narrow streets and alleyways to astonishing balconies overlooking the sea from where the Adriatic and its coastline offer a spectacle unique in the world.

Within the historic center, there are several monuments to visit: the statue of the great Polignano-born singer Domenico Modugno, the church of Santa Maria Assunta in Cielo and the other churches scattered in the various narrow streets, the bridge over Lama Monachile, and the Pino Pascali Museum of Contemporary Art, with several exhibitions inside.

Polignano is worth visiting at any time of the year: events, concerts, festivals, and ceremonies of all kinds are always present. At Christmas, the historic center is decorated and decked out with lights and Christmas motifs.

Let's now consider the picturesque beaches of Polignano, its coastline, and the various caves that make it magnificent:

CALA PORTO or Lama Monachile

We can say that it is the symbolic beach of Polignano. Located just outside the historic center, you can enter it by crossing the ancient Via Traiana bridge.

The small beach, composed of pebbles, is an inlet surrounded by rocky walls overlooked by houses and buildings. A truly picturesque place. It is precisely here that an essential scene of the well-known soap-opera Beautiful was filmed;

Lido Cala Paura

This beach, just over 1 km from the city center, has always escaped mass tourism and is much sought after by those looking for quiet places to relax.

The beach is mainly free, although there is plenty of part of it where access is charged.

It is accessed by a flight of steps carved into the rock, and both the beach and the seabed are rocky.

By moonlight, this small piece of coastline offers an awe-inspiring spectacle, creating a romantic and unforgettable setting;

Cala San Vito

Cala San Vito's free beach in Polignano is a little more than 3.5 kilometers from the city center.

The name is due to the Abbey dedicated to the Saint located nearby, where there is also find an observation tower, a common element along the entire Adriatic coast.

The beach of Cala San Vito in Polignano a Mare is quite wide and mostly rocky, as is the seabed, which turns out to be shallow near the coast. Access is via a footbridge, which facilitates passage to the beach;

Porto Cavallo

Porto Cavallo is a charming free beach located about 3 km from the center of Polignano. It is small and has a sandy part and a more significant part of rocky coastline. The seabed is sandy and shallow. However, moving away from the shore, the water quickly becomes very high. Its location makes it a sheltered place from the winds. To reach it, it is necessary to travel along a narrow, bumpy road;

Cala Fetente

Cala Fetente is one of the enchanting beaches on the coast of Polignano a Mare. It has a free part and a private part. It is very suitable for children, and it is possible to rent beach chairs, umbrellas, and equipment for water sports. The beach has fine, light-colored sand, and the crystal-clear waters are ideal for snorkelers.

THE SEA CAVES

The Caves of Polignano a Mare are a must-see attraction for those visiting the Apulian city.

These underwater caves, famous for the beauty of their colors and shapes, are a popular destination for scuba diving enthusiasts. Visiting them, you cannot help but notice the imaginative shapes assumed by stalactites and stalagmites over the millennia or natural pools that create a unique and fascinating environment. In addition, these caves are important historical sites, as they have been used over the millennia by humans, for example, as places of worship.

As many as 21 caves have been recorded in Polignano, of which these are the most famous.

Grotta Della Rondinella

This cave is so named because tradition tells of a small swallow that nested and hatched its pups inside the cavity.

One year due to a sea storm, the cave was flooded entirely, so swallowed and the pups did not survive.

That is why it is said that if you hear the swallow's cry and swallows on stormy days, doom is impending.

Reaching this cave is easier by sea, while the route is quite difficult by land.

Grotta Ardito

This cave is named after its former owners. At one time, it was possible to access it by a ladder.

Inside the cave is a huge column called the "Column of Hercules," as it gives the impression that it is holding up the whole world from its position.

Grotta Palazzese

The best-known cave in Polignano, as well as being the most remarkable in size. It has been known for centuries, so much so that men like Diderot have spoken of it.

Here, too, there was once a ladder to access its interior.

In the twentieth century, it was transformed, first into a bathing establishment, then into a restaurant overlooking the sea, which is now very popular.

By sea, the cave has two natural entrances leading to a large room, connected to a smaller one with a small pebble beach.

Grotta di Sella

It is characterized by its natural suspension bridge, created after the gradual collapse of the inner part of the sea cave vault.

Grotta delle monache

It was so named because, in the past, the hospital nuns used the small beach nearby without being disturbed.

Grotta dei colombi

In addition to being a nesting place for birds, the cave is also home to significant archaeological findings.

These are just some of the caves in Polignano a mare. There are others, such as the cave of San Lorenzo, Grotta Azzurra, Grotta dei Ladroni, Grotta della foca, and many others.

Many of these can be visited in different ways.

By boat or amphibious vehicle: many of the smaller caves are accessible only by boat or amphibious vehicle, which will allow you to navigate inside the caves;

By organized tour: several agencies organize tours of the caves of Polignano a Mare. Usually, there are also local guides who will explain all the secrets and beauties of the various caves; Independently: here, adventure lovers can indulge themselves. By following prepared paths and signs, it is possible to visit some of the caves independently.

The advice is to check the availability and condition of caves before you go, as some may be closed for conservation or safety reasons.

RED BULL CLIFF DIVING

An event that has now found a home in Polignano is the spectacular Red Bull Clidd Diving.

It takes place a real extreme diving competition in which, some of the most daring to famous athletes in the world, dive from 25 meters high into the blue waters of the Adriatic Sea.

Polignano's stage of this type of competition has proved to be particularly popular with both athletes and spectators, where the spectacular nature of the sport combines with the beauty of the rocky cliffs and white houses directly overlooking the Adriatic, providing a spectacle unique in the world.

FOODS TO ABSOLUTELY ENJOY ON THE ADRIATIC COAST

As for food on the Adriatic coast, there is plenty to indulge in. The list would be very long. However, these are the foods that you cannot help but taste:

Fresh fish: octopus, anchovies, squid, sea urchins, mussels... you name it; served raw as an appetizer, roasted, or cooked in tomato sauce. We are on the coast, and here the catch, in addition to being of excellent quality, is always very fresh.

Focaccia barese: delicious and perfect for breakfast, lunch, dinner, or snacks. Crispy outside and soft inside. Tradition calls for it to be topped with fresh or peeled tomatoes. Enjoy while sitting on the Bari waterfront (but other cities are fine, too) accompanied by a cold beer.

Panzerotti fritti: another must-have. A golden, crispy wrapper contained a combination of mozzarella and tomato sauce. A food as good as few others in the world. Also excellent in its dozens of variations: with ground meat, turnip tops, and ham.

Rice, potatoes, and mussels (tiella): a first course you will never forget. A delicious combination of land and sea elements. Tradition calls for the three main ingredients to be prepared and cooked in the same pan.

Braciole al sugo: slices of veal or horse stuffed seasoned with cheese, salt, and parsley and simmered for hours in tomato sauce. The meat becomes tender and soft, and the flavor is indescribable.

Homemade pasta: Some foods, such as homemade pasta, are found throughout the region, but they take different forms and characteristics depending on the area of reference. In the area of the Adriatic coast and Bari we go for orecchiette and cavatelli (strascinati).

Sgagliozze: fried pieces of polenta, a typical street food to eat while walking through the streets of the old city.

As for wine to go with these dishes, there are several types from the central Adriatic coast.

Arletta red wine: its color is a ruby tending to garnet, with orange highlights emerging as it ages. Its flavor is very dry and full-bodied. Its alcohol content does not exceed 12%.

Moscato di Trani: The grapes for producing this wine are harvested when almost withered. It has a yellow color and a characteristic aroma when aged inside wooden barrels. At the same time, its flavor is sweet, so much so that it is indicated as ideal to accompany dry pastries or delicate desserts.

Aleatico: red wine, very sweet and aromatic. Its aroma is intense and fruity, with notes of cherry and plum. It needs an aging period of a few years to fully develop all its qualities.

CHAPTER 3

THE MURGIA AREA

If you love to discover the hidden secrets of small towns perched on the slopes of rolling hills with their flavors and traditions still intact, or if you want to explore nature with its incredible biodiversity, you must pass through the Murgia area.

The Murgia is an area of karst origin, which characterizes much of the region, whose distinctive elements are hills and plateaus within which caves, canyons, and almost magical places develop.

The Murgia territory spans the entire central Apulian area, from Barletta to the Itria Valley, and includes part of the bordering region of Basilicata, within whose borders are the very famous Sassi di Matera (more on this later).

In this area, the bond with nature is very strong, so much so that there is an effort to promote a form of "slow" tourism, where those who arrive are almost obliged to stop to savor the tranquility, the quietness of these territories, to take a moment to understand the richness of a territory that at first glance may appear unkind, almost arid, and in which it seems impossible that civilizations had managed to develop.

Instead, behind this appearance lies an absolute treasure trove of natural, historical, and cultural riches, with a tradition that in the face of modernity, has been able to renew itself without losing its identity. Therefore, proceeding slowly and stopping, if necessary, is the first step to capturing the essence and beauty of this wonderful corner of Puglia.

Much of the Murgia territory has been included in the "High Murgia National Park" as an area to be valued and protected precisely because of its biodiversity and how man interacted with it.

The first of the places that immediately comes to mind when thinking of the Murgia is Castel del Monte, on the UNESCO heritage list.

CASTEL DEL MONTE

The castle is near Andria, not far from Barletta (about 30 km). It was built by Emperor Frederick II of Swabia on a rocky bank elevated above the surrounding area, over which it dominates with its imposing figure.

Its octagonal plan is unique, with eight towers at its eight vertices, which are themselves octagonal in plan. From whichever angle you look at it, this presents itself as an incredible spectacle that leaves you speechless Just this particular design of its own has caused various legends to arise around the castle: some consider it to be a kind of place of initiation for those who wanted to initiate themselves into elitist knowledge, according to others the castle has the same shape as those that were the emperor's crown. Still, others claim that the Holy Grail was kept in the castle.

Whether these stories are true or not, they indicate how much wonder this beautiful structure, which had a function of defense, but also of recreation and study, has always caused. The emperor regarded it as a place where he could take refuge and devote himself to his passions, such as falconry.

Its importance is such that the effigy of the castle is imprinted on the Italian one-cent coin.

The castle can only be visited by reservation. No more than 30 people are allowed inside at a time.

Inside, it is possible to roam freely around the two floors that make up the castle, as well as the courtyard and the winding spiral staircase found inside the towers.

Car parking is a mile away, and a shuttle bus is available to take you to the foot of the castle if you want to avoid walking.

ALTAMURA

One of the most important centers in the Murgia area is Altamura, a city famous all over the world for its bread, but not only.

Altamura is nicknamed "The Lioness of Apulia" because of its history, importance, and beauty.

At the behest of Frederick II, a splendid cathedral was built here, dedicated to Santa Maria Assunta, with two of its imposing bell towers and the two 16th-century lions placed on either side of the entrance.

The church, as seen today, majestic on the town's main square, is the result of stratifications and interventions over time. Nevertheless, it retains all its splendor as a medieval cathedral, which is well worth a visit.

During the Middle Ages, thanks in particular to the thrust of Frederick II, Altamura became a very important center. We could say cosmopolitan today, where small neighborhoods related to different ethnic groups such as Arabs, Jews or Greeks were created. These neighborhoods correspond to today's historic center in a set of small streets and small, characteristic squares called claustrum.

These small squares are distributed throughout the historic center of Altamura and are evidence of community life. Some of them possessed a well from which the inhabitants could draw water. Their function was also defensive, as this was where enemies who were unlikely to escape could be attracted.

Within these enclosed spaces, it is possible to observe a whole series of loggias, staircases, balconies, and other architectural elements that highlight the coexistence and intermingling of different cultures and ornamental elements different natures carved in the tuff.

Throughout the city's historical center there are about 80 cloisters; it is worth "getting lost" to search these very characteristic places.

But Altamura and its territory also have a history that predates man: here, in fact, about twenty years ago, thousands of dinosaur footprints were discovered in a private area, which are still the result of studies and research.

For the time being, it is possible to visit them only during the period from May to October by reservation, as explained on the website:

https://www.comune.altamura.ba.it/index.php/it/novita/ notizie/item/1215-prenotazioni-e-visite-guidate-alla-cava-dei- dinosauri-linee-guida-e-modulo

Staying still in ancient times, Altamura was the site of an incredible discovery: inside the cave of Lamalunga, a complete skeleton was found, dating back to a man who lived hundreds of thousands of years ago and according to recent estimates, classifiable as Neanderthal man.

The exceptionality of the find lies in the fact that the entire human structure has come down to us in an exceptional state of preservation, thanks to the gradual "incorporation" of the body by the surrounding rocks.

These remains are still there where they were found. Removing them is impossible, even though this possibility has been discussed for a long time.

It is precisely around this find that a museum circuit has sprung up, which also allows us to understand the nature and history of the Murgia area:

- The Lamalunga visitor center: about 3 km from the village, from which an exciting journey to discover the area and how Neanderthals came to be discovered. This is also the privileged point to set off in search of extraordinary places, such as "the bat room," where you can experience echolocation, that is, orienting yourself and understanding the presence of obstacles through ultrasound.

- Palazzo Baldassare: In this splendid palace built between the 16th and 17th

centuries, an itinerary has been created that has as its theme the evolution of man, the times, and ways in which it occurred, with the support of various instruments. Of course, special attention is given to the "Man of Altamura," so much so that in the palace, there is a full-scale reconstruction of the place where the skeleton was found and where it is still preserved today.

• National Archaeological Museum: here, the temporal experience is broader in the sense that the historical path covered goes from the Stone Age to the Middle Ages. Thanks to various computer and multimedia aids, prehistoric men's mentalities and ways of life are explained. So, again starting from the "Altamura Man," we go on an incredible journey to discover the life of hundreds of thousands of years ago.

THE PULO OF ALTAMURA

Not far from the area of the incredible discovery of prehistoric man, there is another special place: the Pulo of Altamura. As already mentioned, we must consider that being an area of essentially limestone origin, the whole of Murgia is full of caves, sinkholes, and all those phenomena typical of such an area.

Compared to Molfetta, the Pulo di Altamura presents a maximum depth of 75 meters with a diameter of 500 m. Along its walls are several caves that help to understand how water erosion works and reveal much about local history, as these caves have been inhabited since prehistoric times.

The place is truly enchanting, and if you wish, you can descend thanks to some trails with proper precautions.

Several agencies organize excursions and treks to discover the wonders of the Pulo area.

For climbing lovers, climbing the steep walls of the Pulo is also possible. However, it is only possible to do so between September and December. This is because the kestrel falcon nests here, and from January to August, climbing is prohibited, precisely to protect the broods of these birds.

THE BREAD OF ALTAMURA

Finally, we cannot talk about Altamura without considering what its crowning achievement is from a gastronomic point of view and beyond: its bread, famous and exported worldwide.

To understand why this bread is so good, you have to do only one thing: taste it.

This bread has a crispy crust, while inside it is soft and fluffy. A simple flavor, but one that warms your heart, accompanied perhaps by a drizzle of oil, also produced locally, or made into bruschetta, a slice of toasted bread seasoned with oil, salt, and a light rub of garlic, maybe accompanied by a good glass of wine.

The recipe for this bread has been unchanged for centuries: durum wheat flour, sourdough starter, salt, and water. These ingredients are enough to bring to life what is considered the best bread in the world. While it is baking, after a processing and rising phase, it must take place in a wood-fired oven on a stone base. Hundreds-years-old ovens still operate in the city and follow the ancient recipe.

A bread museum is available today to understand what bread represents for Altamura and the context in which it was created. This has been set up in one of the old ovens in the town, where through a multi- media and sensory journey, one will realize the strong connection of bread production with the surrounding area.

GRAVINA AND THE RUPESTRIAN CIVILIZATION

A short distance from Altamura is another incredible village where it seems that time has stopped: Gravina in Puglia.

In fact, the entire village rises on a "gravina," one of those typical canyons of the Murgia, which contributes to creating a fairy-tale land- atmosphere, a sort of gateway to an enchanted world.

Human presence in this area has been attested since prehistoric times; in fact, there are several archaeological sites surrounding the Gravina area.

For a long time, the niches distributed along the canyon were used as houses or shelters in case of danger, most of which can be visited today.

Many of these cave environments are carved deep into the rock, such as the cave of the seven chambers. These include precious rock churches such as the crypt of San Vito Vecchio and the church of San Michele delle Grotte.

A symbol of the city is the aqueduct bridge, famous as it appeared in the latest film in the Secret Agent 007 saga, which connects the two banks of the Gravina and is 37 meters high.

UNDERGROUND GRAVINA

Underground Gravina is a beautiful treasure hidden from the surface: a sequence of environments, spaces, rock churches, and narrow meanders that develop under the city, completely excavated by hand. An incredible spectacle. If you happen to be in these areas, all you can do is leave the sunlight behind and enter this "alternative" world to the surface, where time seems not to exist.

To visit underground Gravina, you need to make reservations and choose which route to follow. Several options are available, with different routes and times. This is the website for all the information:

https://www.gravinasotterranea.it/

Coming back up, a visit to the magnificent old town is to be noticed. Consisting of three wards, it represents the old part overlooking the canyon end, with a panoramic tour as beautiful as any.

Having been over time a town with some importance (there was even a pope originally from this hamlet), the historic center of Gravina is teeming with noble palaces and churches, buildings constructed from white tuff, a typical local stone.

ST. GIORGIO'S FAIR

Gravina is also famous for hosting what is considered the oldest fair in the world, it has even been held since 1294!

Today the fair opens with a magnificent medieval re-enactment through which a precise ritual is retraced, as it took place centuries ago. Nothing could be more evocative and exciting. The fair itself involves the whole town. It is not only composed of exhibitors who intend to sell their wares or who want to showcase the latest news and trends of the moment but also presents concerts, and events of all kinds in which everyone, citizens and non-citizens, are called upon to participate.

The event usually takes place in the second half of April and lasts just under a week. Ready to throw yourself into an ocean of colors, sounds, and fun?

CASTELLANA CAVES

Caves and underground cavities are scattered almost everywhere in an area composed of limestone rocks, and it is no coincidence that the largest and most spectacular cave complex, spanning 3 km in length, is located in the very area we are about to talk about.

In the province of Bari, not far from Polignano, is the town of Castellana Grotte, which owes its name precisely to the presence of this cave complex candidate for UNESCO World Heritage status.

The Castellana Caves are among the most famous underground natural cavities in the world, and since they were opened to the public, more than 15 million people have visited them. Visiting the caves is a 3-kilometer route that takes visitors 70 meters deep into an extraordinary environment that no wildest imagination could imagine. Here canyons, deep chasms, fossilizations, stalactites, stalagmites, and concretions surprise children and adults alike. Therefore, these caves are an unmissable opportunity to admire one of Puglia's most extraordinary natural places.

To visit the caves, it is possible to make the ticket online and onsite. Of course, the walk in the caves is always under the guidance of experienced staff who know the place. A short and a long route are available,and it is also possible, by reservation, to visit the caves at night.

To further appreciate the beauty of the place, concerts, theater events, and exhibitions have also been organized inside the caves for the past few years.

One example is the show "Hell in the Cave," where a theatrical performance of the cantica of Hell from the Divine Comedy by Dante Alighieri, the supreme Italian poet, is put on.

Hell in the Cave is a theatrical performance that uses the Castellana Caves as a natural setting. The event combines dance, voices, sounds, and lights in a grand multimedia performance that transports the audience on an adventure into Hell as described by Dante. The natural environment of the caves is transformed into a stage of macroscopic dimensions, and the audience is captured by the innovative theatrical dynamics that lead them into a unique experience in Hell.

PUTIGNANO AND ITS CARNIVAL

If in Gravina we find the oldest fair in the world, the city of Putignano is home to the oldest carnival in Europe.

Here the carnival is a deeply felt event, the preparations for which last most of the year. It begins in December with the so-called offshoots and continues until "Shrove Tuesday," the day before "Ash Wednesday," with which the period of Lent begins.

The Putignano carnival (held according to tradition in the weeks preceding Lent), takes place through really special festivities and rituals, finding the highest and best-known expression in its four parades, three on Sundays, the last one corresponding to Shrove Tuesday.

When one thinks of the Putignano carnival, the papier-mâché giants immediately rush to one's mind: huge sculptures (called floats) made by the skilled hands of papier-mâché artisans, which are distinguished by their refinement, workmanship, and finish, the technique of which is handed down from master to master.

Carnival in Putignano has been celebrated as far back as 1394.

Those were years when foreign peoples carried out constant attacks and raids on the Adriatic coast. There was a particular fear of the theft of the holy relics in case of attacks.

It was then decided to transfer the remains of the protomartyr Stephen from Monopoli to the best-defended Putignano church, that of Santa Maria la Greca.

With a procession, the transfer of the remains took place on St. Stephen's Day itself. It is from this moment that history fades into legend:

> *Oral tradition has it that peasants performing grafts on vines, according to the technique known as "off-shooting," at the sight of the procession abandoned their activity and followed it with singing, dancing, and satirical verses.* ❧

This is the best-known story about the origins of Europe's oldest and longest-running carnival and the festival from which it all began, that of the offshoots.

So, for a long time, the Carnival was a festival the preserve of the peasantry, in which ideally, roles in society were reversed, and the wealthier classes were somehow mocked.

It was not until the 1930s that the carts created with straw and rags began to give way to floats made of iron and papier-mâché, making the Carnival a celebration in which all walks of life participated. From the 1950s onward, thanks to new techniques and materials, floats took on the complexity and beauty that can still be admired today. Floats that are always related to current political and economic events intrinsically carry a message that never gets old.

The atmosphere of the Putignano carnival is incredible. The preparations of the costumes, masks, floats, parades and rituals repeated every year reinforce the sense of a community that welcomes everyone, inviting them to participate in a celebration of exaggerated fun.

PATHS AND TRAILS OF MURGIA

The Murgia is a wonderful territory. Therefore, the "Alta Murgia National Park" entity was established precisely to protect its flora and fauna and to best preserve all the treasures of the small villages. The goal is also to enhance all this magnificent territory offers.

For those who want to enjoy and get to know the Murgia in its most natural, wildest aspect, several itineraries can be followed, depending on your strength and desire to explore. Such itineraries can last from a few hours to several days, with development in stages, to be done for example, on foot or even by bike.

In these itineraries, you can get to know more closely what is the typical flora of the place, such as oaks or olive trees, but also wildlife, such as the birds of prey typical of these places, or the jazzi, those structures used by shepherds to aggregate their herds.

An example of an itinerary is the Jazzo Rosso-San Magno-Castel del Monte cycle route, which includes seven routes for a total of 65 kilometers, which can be done either on foot or by bike. At the same time, some of these stretches can also be done on horseback.

In recent years, many associations and groups have been organizing itineraries linking various cities in Puglia and beyond.

One such itinerary starts in Bari with a week-long route in stages along the Murgia Mountains to reach one of the unique UNESCO heritages in the world: the city of Matera and its world-famous Sassi.

THE CITY OF STONES: MATERA

Before talking about Matera, it is necessary to specify how it, despite being part of the Basilicata region, is located in a purely Murgia geographical territory, therefore with features in common with the area we have treated so far. Moreover, given the geographical proximity, it is impossible not to talk about a unique place in the world.

Matera is a city that leaves anyone who visits it speechless, attracting tourists worldwide thanks to its beauty and cultural heritage. Declared a UNESCO World Heritage Site, this city offers a lot to see, such as natural areas, museums, rock churches, and breathtaking landscapes.

But let's start with why Matera deserves so much attention. What are these Sassi?

By Sassi we mean an actual city totally carved out of the rock. Houses, churches, water wells, and any kind of structure or building have been carved out by digging everything by hand over time. In an overpopulated and very poor hygienic conditions, these environments were inhabited until a few decades ago, so much so that a nationwide scandal was created that forced the government to intervene and move those who lived inside these "caves."

Later, after a few years of total neglect, these environments were recovered and restored, showing themselves to the world in all their splendor and uniqueness.

The area of the Sassi is divided into two areas, that of the Sasso Caveoso, which houses the oldest part, and that of the Sasso Barisano whose original core has been gradually modified over time, with houses no longer dug into the rock but built.

It is difficult to explain the beauty of this city if you do not see it in person because it almost seems as if it has been transplanted to the present day directly from another era or even from another world.

Taking a walk through these ancient little streets, made up of stairs, narrow streets, blind alleys, and balconies overlooking nowhere, is an experience that gives emotions that, in terms of intensity and uniqueness, cannot be found anywhere else.

Among the many places in Matera to visit, there are a couple that are able to give an insight into the identity and authenticity of Matera:

- The church of Madonna of Idris: it is recognizable as being dug into a small mound with an iron cross on top, one of the most beautiful rock-hewn churches, partly dug into the rock, built, both because of its panoramic position and the fact that it is very ancient and has within its small environment frescoes of Byzantine origin.

- Vico Solitario Cave House: a cave-house showing how a peasant society lived until a few decades ago. It is not far from the Church of Our Lady of Idris.

The Cave House is furnished exactly as it would have been back in time. It allows us to understand how a poor, mostly peasant population lived here, with the space dedicated to animals, the water collection system, and all the everyday items used at the time. Something that seems incredible today.

Matera's treasures are countless; listing them all here would be impossible. However, among those that definitely remain in the soul of those who visit are:

- The church of St. Augustine was built on the top of a spur, on what is called the "Belvedere of the Murgia." Its style is typically Baroque, while inside, at 2 euros, it is possible to visit a cave church with several frescoes. A place steeped in history with a very characteristic setting, The cathedral of Matera, dedicated to the holy Madonna della Bruna and St. Eustace, a triumph of Baroque with stucco and decorations that make it a beautiful place. The cathedral is located at the city's highest point, and to reach it you will have to walk up climbs, stairs, and small paths... but both the walk and the view of both the church and the surrounding area will be worth it.

- Underground Matera, an actual city under the city. Composed of streets, houses, warehouses, stables, barns, lighting, and ventilation systems placed below the surface creates a mystical atmosphere which breathes the essence of ancient times and civilizations.

- The long Palombaro, a large cistern connected by canals to underground tunnels once used to collect rainwater, shows the capacity for ingenuity and adaptation to an often-hostile place of the ancient population of Matera. It descends to a depth of 17 meters to admire one of the largest stone-cut cisterns in the world.

- The many rock-hewn churches, hermitages, and small religious environments carved into the rock, for which tours are also provided.

As mentioned, these are just some beauties that await you in Matera.

For those who want to discover the history and traditions of Matera further, there are several museums in the city, both public and private, that can give you an understanding of the more than thousand-year history of this area.

FEAST OF THE MADONNA DELLA BRUNA

The last special feature to highlight is the patronal feast, which takes place in early July: on the evening of the feast, a huge cavalcade precedes a large papier-mâché float that carries the Madonna della Bruna, the saint patron of Matera, around the city.

At the end of the parade, there comes the moment that all the people of Matera look forward to with trepidation: the destruction of the float. Instead, everyone pounces on it to take home a piece of the choreography of the float as a symbol of good luck and blessing. Something in which the sacred and the profane merge, creating a completely incredible moment that is both wonderful and frightening at the same time.

There are several legends as to the reason for this tradition, one of which speaks of an attack by the Saracens and the decision by the people of Matera to destroy the effigy of the Madonna to keep it from falling into enemy hands, or another that speaks of disagreements between the local lord, Count Tramontano, hated by the people of Matera, who following a rebellion had made several promises to appease their tempers, including that of guaranteeing a new float every year for the patronal feast.

The citizens then destroyed the float to make the count keep his promise.

Whatever the truth may be, the patronal feast casts a charge of joy, colors, lights and fun over the town to which all are invited, where preparations are made to welcome all those who want to share an atmosphere of celebration and merriment.

FOODS TO ABSOLUTELY ENJOY IN THE MURGIA AREA

Except for fresh fish, the foods in the Murgia area are similar to those found in Bari environs. Also, in the Murgia, focaccia, panzerotti, fresh pasta, and many other products we have already mentioned are found everywhere.

This area is particularly characterized by the production of cheeses and dairy products, both fresh and aged.

Other elements of the local cuisine are legumes, such as chickpeas, chickling peas, and beans.

Essential for typical dishes are wild herbs such as chicory, sivoni, asparagus, and other plants that grow wild, used to prepare tasty and genuine dishes or as side dishes.

In each center of the Murgia area, it is possible to taste a specialty typical only of that particular center.

Altamura bread: we have already described Altamura bread, its authenticity, and the importance it has achieved.

Pallone of Gravina: pallone of Gravina is a semi-hard, spherical- shaped cheese made from raw cow's milk cheese. It has different aging times. it is considered one of the finest cheeses in southern Italy.

Andria's burrata: this is a fresh cheese made from cow's milk. It looks like a pouch whose interior is filled with a mixture of cream and shreds of the same paste used for the wrapping. The flavor is exceptional because of its softness and uniqueness.

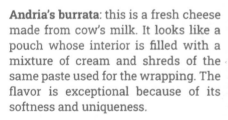

Pecora alla pignatta (cutturidd): a typical Matera dish, widespread throughout the Murgia area, where it takes on different names depending on where it is eaten. It is a lamb stew, simmered for hours in an earthenware pot with many ingredients, especially the wild herbs typical of the Murgia, such as chicory and asparagus.

Eating this lamb stew is a return to the flavors of yesteryear, those of the peasant civilization, to something extremely simple, but that has nothing to envy from more modern and emblazoned dishes.

Peperoni cruschi: these are another Matera specialty. The peppers are deep red and particularly prized for their sweetness. "Crusco" stands for crunchy, which is the typical characteristic of these peppers, which lend themselves to be cooked in many different ways, eaten as a snack or as a side dish for other dishes.

As for wines, we find many noteworthy products here as well.

Castel del Monte: this wine is one of the most famous in the entire Murgia area. It is a very popular wine in its white version and the other red and rosé versions. It is very dry and fresh on the palate.

Primitivo di Gioia del Colle: wine produced for centuries in the Murgia area. It presents a very intense ruby-red color, almost purplish.

Its flavor is very warm and enveloping, with a robust fruity component.

Gravina: White wine, suitable for mushrooms or fish. Its appearance is straw-colored, tending to soft green, while it is dry or sweetish on the palate. It is also produced in a sparkling version.

CHAPTER 4

ITRIA VALLEY AND THE TRULLI AREA

Located in the most southern part of the Murgia, the Itria Valley, also called the valley of the trulli, is located in the area roughly compressed between the chief towns of Bari, Taranto, and Brindisi.

The Itria Valley is, according to all, simply stunning. With its expanses of olive trees, towns characterized by the whiteness of the houses, ancient farms, and yet another UNESCO heritage site in Apulia, the trulli of Alberobello, it guarantees an unforgettable spectacle for all tourists who visit it.

All the elements that can be found in this succession of gentle highlands contribute to the fairy-tale atmosphere that is worth being surrounded by at least once in a lifetime.

The Itria Valley villages have long been considered among the most beautiful in Italy. They are places full of life, where events with international resonance take place, and where unique traditions and flavors can be found.

There are no more Instagrammable places than those in the Itria Valley.

But let's start on this journey by beginning with the most famous of these villages: Alberobello.

ALBEROBELLO

Despite being an increasingly popular destination, especially for mass tourism, this small village manages to retain all its charm and magic.

Its outline is delineated by quite distinctive dwellings, built with local stones and set together without cement or mortar, according to the technique known as "a secco." The conical roof is characteristic, composed of "chiancarelle" with the keystone surmounted by

a pinnacle, which can take different shapes, and according to tradition, serves to drive away bad luck. For the same reason, a religious or mythological symbol is painted on each of these roofs with white ash.

To wander into the trulli area, with its alleys full of flowers, artisans, restaurants, and with the smells of typical Apulian cuisine, is to end up in a fairy tale, in a labyrinth that is the result of some magician's imagination.

These are the must-see spots within the trulli area:

- Trullo Sovrano, located in the northern part of town, the only double-floor Trullo in Alberobello furnished with original furniture from the early 20th century;
- The Monti district, the largest area of trulli. Here are the two Siamese Trulli, two trulli with their cones fused centrally, which, according to an old tradition, are the symbol of a troubled history between two brothers;
- "Casa Pezzolla," where 15 communicating trulli constitute a museum that tells the story of the area, which can be visited free of charge.

Finally, if you want an unforgettable souvenir photo, go to Belvedere Santa Lucia for the best view of the whole trulli complex. The advice is to go there at sunset, because the view is very impressive.

LOCOROTONDO

While Alberobello is famous for the conical shape of the roofs of its houses, Locorotondo is renowned for its "cummerse." In short, the stone used is the same as that seen in Alberobello. However, the roofs are pitched and aligned with the walls of the fronts. Were it not for the difference in the materials used, the houses in Locorotondo would be quite similar to typical houses in northern European countries. The shape of these roofs is functional for rainwater collection.

The village of Locorotondo is distinguished by its circular layout (thus its name) and historic center, with white walls and colorful flowers everywhere, making the narrow streets a fairy-tale place.

SAN GIORGIO CHURCH

The Mother Church of St. George is the main place of worship in the village and is located in the heart of the historic center. With its 35- meter-high dome and bell tower standing above the other buildings, the church is easily visible even from a distance.

The church was built between 1790 and 1825 and is based on the remains of two older churches dating back to 1195 and the 16th century, respectively. The facade of the church follows a majestic and elegant 16th-century style. At the same time, the interior has a cross-shaped plan and is characterized by a fusion of elements of Baroque and Renaissance architecture. Inside the church is a painting of St. George and a magnificent marble altar.

ST NICOLA CHURCH

A more hidden and modest church, but one with a magnificently frescoed ceiling, is the Church of St. Nicholas, built in the 1600s. Inside there are also stone bas-reliefs found inside a cave, presumed, therefore, to be older than the church itself, depicting the crucifixion of Jesus.

Locorotondo also turns out to be magnificent because of the natural setting in which it stands: from its position, it dominates the entire Itria Valley, offering breathtaking views.

In this regard, it is a must to reach the viewpoint of Lungovalle - Via Nardelli - Lungomare. Many beautiful venues here allow you to have a few drinks while overlooking a magnificent view.

Of all the events that are organized in this beautiful village, the Locus festival is a music festival that hosts famous international artists every year, varying for multiple musical genres.

MARTINA FRANCA

The triumph of Baroque characterizes Martina Franca. We find this architectural style throughout the historic center, coexisting alongside the trulli, also present here.

Among the churches to visit, San Martino is considered an important example of Baroque architecture in union with local elements. It is precisely the appearance of this and other churches in the historic center and beyond that contributes to the visually spectacular appearance of this village.

Instead, in the splendid Ducal Palace, it is possible to

visit two museums: one dedicated to a particular theme, the forest (in the territory of Martina Franca falls the Pianelle forest, considered a nature reserve), while the other is an exhibition of contemporary art.

Finally, not far from Martina Franca, in its magnificent countryside, is the cave of Mount Fellone, inside which tools dating back to the Neolithic period have been found. It is certainly worth a visit.

ITRIA VALLEY FESTIVAL

For music lovers, Martina Franca has been home to the "Festival della Valle d'Itria," a major cultural event held every summer to promote music and culture in the Itria Valley region, managing to attract visitors from all over the world.

The festival, which takes place during July and August, as the title says, is held in Martina Franca and nearby towns such as Locorotondo, Cisternino, and Ostuni. The festival's programming mainly includes performances of opera, ballet, and classical music, with the participation of internationally renowned artists.

This festival has become famous due to its productions of rare and little-performed operas, such as some of the works of Gioachino Rossini, a native of the Itria Valley region. In addition to concerts, the festival also offers events such as art exhibitions, meetings with artists, film screenings, and other cultural events.

The Itria Valley Festival is a unique experience for music and culture lovers and offers the chance to discover the beauty of this area.

Especially classical music lovers cannot miss the opportunity to attend this important cultural event.

OSTUNI

Now let's talk about Ostuni, the "White City of Apulia," so called because of its historic center characterized by houses and buildings painted with white lime. The color was not chosen casually: first of all, white lime is very easy to find in the area, then the color gives more light to the narrow and winding streets of the historic center, and finally, it was a widespread belief that white lime was a natural disinfectant against the Plague.

Ostuni stands on three hills, and compared to other towns in the Itria Valley, it is close to the sea.

To visit it is to be thunderstruck by this village that, from its position, dominates the entire surrounding area.

Ostuni is graceful and wandering through its incredible historic center's narrow, white streets. So, you can understand how this small town annually attracts thousands of tourists from all over the globe.

Many routes can be followed within the historic center. However, the advice of those who have been there is to walk freely and marvel at every corner, every glimpse, every beautiful church that suddenly appears before you, and squares filled with craft stores and restaurants that will make your mouth water.

PIAZZA DELLA LIBERTA'

A must-see is " Piazza della libertà," the main square, where St. Francis Palace, a former monastery and now a city palace, stands out, with the beautiful St. Francis Church next to it. This square is always full of people, movement, and places to relax and enjoy the view. But its beauty does not end there.

In the center of the square stands a 21-meter-high obelisk with the statue of the city's patron saint, St. Oronzo, on top.

Finally, in this square, it is possible to observe the archaeological excavation that has unearthed part of the city's ancient fortifications, the construction of which predates 1500.

THE DEFENSIVE BELTS

There are 3 imposing defensive walls around the city, each referring to a particular historical period: the first was built by the Messapians, a very ancient population of the place; the second by the Byzantine emperor Basil the Macedonian; and the last, the most majestic is the one built by the Aragonese, whose archaeological excavation is visible in Piazza della Libertà.

THE COAST NEAR OSTUNI

Let's put aside the beauty of the historic center to head toward the sea. Ostuni is also famous for this.

The center is only 8 km from the Adriatic coast, where the sea is clean, transparent, and unspoiled, and the beaches and coves are a wonder of nature, particularly on the Costa Merlata. The Ostuni marina has 20 km of coastline with beautiful and distinctive landscapes. Among those to absolutely visit are:

BEACH OF TORRE Guaceto

This beach is located in the WWF-managed marine protected area of the same name in the municipality of Carovigno, just 8 km from the white city. It is one of the most beautiful in the entire region. The beach takes its name from the nearby Aragonese watchtower and is surrounded by centuries-old olive groves that produce extra virgin olive oil of exceptional quality. The sand on the beach is fine and clear, with golden shades, and the sea is crystal clear with a seabed rich in flora and fauna.

Since the Torre Guaceto area is a natural park, some parts of the beach are not accessible. However, there is plenty of bathing establishments, restaurants, bars, and free areas to relax and enjoy the sea and the scent of the Mediterranean scrub. In addition, there is also a sailing center that offers catamaran, sailing, and windsurfing courses.

Rosa Marina Beach

With its wide expanses of sand, this resort is perfect for families, couples, and young people looking for a dream vacation surrounded by fragrant Mediterranean scrub. Rosa Marina is home to a residential village built in the 1960s that attracts many tourists yearly.

The beach boasts the prestigious 5 Sails Blue Flag from Legambiente and is ideal for lovers of water sports such as windsurfing and kitesurfing. It also offers equipped lidos for renting umbrellas, sunbeds, deckchairs, and villas for rent near the sea for a relaxing stay. This enchanting place is a perfect choice for spending a relaxing vacation away from the hustle and bustle of the hottest resorts.

Santa Sabina Tower

Torre Santa Sabina, located in the so-called Alto Salento, is a beach that offers moments of serenity and relaxation, ideal for those who do not like crowded beaches.

The beach, among the most beautiful on the Brindisi coast, is characterized by cliffs, white sand, and crystal-clear sea, perfect for swimming, while the shallow waters are ideal for children. It is located 15 km from Ostuni.

Torre Santa Sabina, precisely because of the presence of both sand and cliffs, lends itself to the needs of all visitors, including free beaches for the adventurous and numerous bathing establishments for those seeking comfort. Popular beaches include:

- Gola, with high and cliffs, ideal for those who enjoy diving; Camerini, with shallow and sandy seabed ideal for families with children;
- Cavallo Beach, with a horse-shaped rock and the imposing presence of a watchtower;
- Mezzaluna Beach, which offers both free and equipped stretches.

Torre Santa Sabina is a beautiful location, often overlooked in favor of other locations, but able to offer an authentic experience to tourists.

Torre Pozzelle

Torre Pozzelle is a wild and little-known beach in the Ostuni area.

Accessible only on foot after walking along an unpaved path, it consists of several coves, some with sand and others with rocks.

The beach is characterized by its crystal-clear sea and the presence of a 16th-century coastal tower, now partially collapsed. There is little human hand in the Torre Pozzelle area, which is ideal for those who love the wilderness and want to spend moments of relaxation and tranquility.

Costa Merlata

Costa Merlata beach, located near Ostuni, is characterized by fascinating bays alternating sand and jagged rocks overlooking the deep blue Adriatic Sea. The beach's name comes from the jagged shape of the coastline, which is reminiscent of the battlements of medieval castles.

This area offers a peaceful corner away from the hustle and bustle of mass tourism.

Surrounded by Mediterranean vegetation, Costa Merlata is a natural gem perfect for those who love to experience the sea authentically, between rocks and soft sand. The beach is ideal for families and friends seeking relaxation and direct contact with nature.

Are you still there? What are you waiting for? Come immediately to discover these fantastic places!

FOODS TO ABSOLUTELY ENJOY IN THE ITRIA VALLEY

Like the rest of the region, the Itria Valley offers unique and genuine flavors.

The valley's best dishes are made with meat, cooked in wood-fired ovens, and seasoned with spices and herbs. Also of great value is the production of cured meats.

BOMBETTE DI ALBEROBELLO: also called bombette pugliesi, are an incredible treat. Small rolls of pork capocollo seasoned with salt, pepper, and, if needed, a small piece of caciocavallo cheese. Once you taste the first one, you won't be able to stop.

Gnummareddi: these are roulades prepared from mixed offal of lamb and suckling kid, tightened with their own casing along with a parsley leaf. They have a very intense flavor, especially when grilled with bay or olive leaves. They are also found in other areas of Puglia, in different variations and with different names.

Capocollo di Martina Franca: typical cured meat from the Itria Valley, one of the most popular. It is made by subjecting the pig's cervical area to salting, smoking, and then curing. It is a product in high demand everywhere and with extraordinary flavor.

As for wines, we also have a fairly important production here. They stand out in particular:

Vino Locorotondo: is a white wine to be served fresh, ideal as an aperitif.

It is bright greenish in color, with a slightly fruity but intense bouquet. On the palate, it is smooth and with great finesse.

Vino Terra d'Otranto: produced in 3 variants, white, red and rosé.

It is a very versatile wine that goes well with different dishes of Apulian cuisine. It is fresh and light on the palate with a fruity aroma.

Vino Ostuni: Ostuni wine has an intense ruby red color, a complex, and pronounced bouquet, with notes of berries and spices. The palate is full-bodied and tannic, with good structure and long persistence.

CHAPTER 5

SALENTO

With Salento, we have come to the extreme part of Puglia, the southernmost, a peninsula that witnesses the contact between the Ionian and Adriatic Seas.

Salento, because of its traditions, its local languages (in some inland areas, a dialect very similar to ancient Greek, called "Griko," is spoken), and its characteristics is almost considered a different region from the rest of Apulia.

It is an exceptional territory, which almost seems to be born from the union of the sea and the countryside. Yet, despite the strong passion for the sea of the area's inhabitants, even its inland part with the countryside, centuries-old olive trees, vineyards, rhythms, and traditions, has left a strong imprint on the identity of Salento.

From the ancient "masserie", places of dwelling and agricultural production, to the many but very small seaside villages, each with its own story to tell, Salento is ready to leave a part of its magic in the hearts and minds of those who visit it.

A saying in Salento dialect goes like this: "Salentu: lu sule, lu mare, lu ientu" (Salento: the sun, the sea, the wind).

These are the first 3 elements ready to welcome the tourist, seen as a guest to be welcomed and pampered. The sun, ready to embrace its warmth, the sea with its crystal-clear waters like few other places in the world, and the wind that brings with it the typical smells and flavors of these areas.

LECCE

The most important city in Salento is Lecce, the capital of the province and a magnificent example of Baroque architecture.

Starting in the XVII century, architects and artists gave the city that triumphal and majestic appearance that has come down to the present day.

The Baroque physiognomy that characterizes the city today is also made possible by 'the use of local

stone, known as "Pietra leccese." This material of limestone origin is easily worked, and over time tends to take on a typical yellow color, as well as hardening. This stone makes the entire historical center a triumph of putti, twisted elements, garlands, and all that is whimsy and irregularity, making Lecce Baroque an architectural style with clearly recognizable peculiarities.

ST. ORONZO PLAZA

Piazza Sant'Oronzo, one of the most fascinating places in Lecce, fully expresses the city's thousand-year history. Here it is possible to see elements of different eras overlapping and coexisting. The square is an exclusively pedestrian area, so much so that it has become a place where events and manifestations take place, as well as a meeting and entertainment place for the inhabitants of Lecce.

Among the first elements that stand out and characterize Piazza Sant'Oronzo is a portion of the Roman amphitheater brought to light in the 1900s. It is estimated that it could hold up to 25,000 people in its heyday.

Just as in Ostuni, here we have a 29-m column topped by a bronze statue of St. Oronzo, the city's patron saint.

To further embellish the square's beauty and centrality, we have several splendid civil and religious buildings:

- The Sedile (once the seat of the municipality)
- The small church of San Marco
- The church of Santa Maria delle Grazie and Palazzo Carafa

All this view should be considered the "antechamber" to the historical center, the main focus of which is Piazza Duomo, with its magnificent cathedral, bell tower, episcope, and seminary.

PIAZZA DUOMO AND CATHEDRAL

The square hides a series of incredible peculiarities: one of the few squares closed on three sides, with a single entrance. This can be explained by the fact that where there is now access with the presence of propylaea, surmounted by statues depicting three church fathers on one side and St. Irene, St. Oronzo, and St. Venera on the other, there was actually a wall with doors that were locked at night. The whole area of the cathedral constituted a citadel under religious control, autonomous from the rest of the town.

As it appears today, the square with the cathedral and the other buildings is one of the highest expressions of Lecce Baroque: an entire complex of buildings that are harmonious as a whole.

Thanks to the use of yellow-colored Lecce stone for both the buildings and the paving, the square gives back a strong sense of warmth, resulting in a welcoming place for anyone who spends time admiring it.

The greatest wonder, however, comes during sunset: in fact, the sun's rays hitting the protrusions, recesses, and decorations of the façades provide a majestic spectacle of light and shadow, of astounding beauty.

The cathedral has a peculiarity: its façade overlooking Piazza Duomo, which immediately catches the attention of those who arrive, is actually a secondary façade, as it is located on one of the long sides of the church. The main facade, on the other hand, is hidden from the square.

If outside the cathedral presents this bizarre character, entirely "normal" within a Baroque context, the church's interior is no less so.

Decorations and ornaments will leave you breathless, as the whole church is decorated whimsically, with ornaments, architectural solutions, and other devices in front of which one cannot remain indifferent. There are as many as 12 altars besides the main altar, each dedicated to a saint and richly decorated with different motifs.

BELL TOWER IN PIAZZA DUOMO

The architectural complex of Piazza Duomo culminates in the majestic Bell Tower, one of the tallest in Europe, located on the left side of the square. Standing 68 meters tall, the Bell Tower looms lightly in the Lecce sky, dominating the entire historic center with its soaring bulk. It has a square plan with five floors that decrease in height as you ascend, each of which is decorated with a richly ornamented balustrade and a round-arched window. Each floor has a commemorative epitaph at the top. In addition, the top floor features four floral spires on angular obelisks, which correspond to the pinnacles with flowering baskets on the octagonal dome that harmoniously concludes the building.

The bell tower also offers one of the most beautiful views imaginable.

Indeed, you can climb to its top to embrace in a single glance the entire surrounding area all the way to the Adriatic, and on clear days you can even spot the lands of Albania - an incredible sight.

To enjoy this view, walking up many uphill steps was necessary. Today, however, an elevator has been installed that makes it possible to climb to the top of the building effortlessly, subject to ticket payment.

Little trivia: the bell tower is not perfectly straight, but due to a small subsidence of the foundation, it has a slight curve to the left.

EPISCOPE AND SEMINARY

The other two buildings contributing to the harmonious spectacle of Cathedral Square are the bishop's seat, the episcope, and the seminary, which has a highly decorated facade arranged in three orders. Once inside, after passing among 12 statues depicting doctors of the church, a small masterpiece of Baroque art is located in the atrium: a beautifully sculpted "baldachin" well.

A small but very precious treasure to be discovered.

Inside the palace, there is also a museum of sacred art and a small private church dedicated to St. Gregory the Wonderworker, a small treasure chest of Baroque art, unfortunately unknown to many but absolutely worth visiting.

THE CHURCH OF SANTA CROCE

Not far from Piazza Duomo stands a church considered among the masterpieces of all Baroque art: the church of Santa Croce. Built on a pre-existing structure, the church is notable for its intricate decoration both on the facade, with statues, balustrades, indentations, projections, and symbols of various kinds, and on the interior, which is also richly decorated and apt to enrapture anyone who enters.

UNDERGROUND LECCE

An excellent environment that few people know about is the underground Lecce. Like many other Apulian cities, we have discussed, Lecce has its own underground part.

The discovery was accidental, thanks to a private individual who, to carry out pipe replacement work, discovered by chance this hidden world under his house.

Exploration and restoration works have wrested from the oblivion of time incredible places, such as houses, or ancient monasteries, and even tanks in which the Jewish community of Lecce performed their rituals.

To learn more, one can visit and inquire at the "Pheasant Archaeological Museum," housed in that very house from where the discovery started.

OTRANTO

Otranto is the city referred to as the "Gateway to the East" since among the Italian countries, it is the one that is located most eastward, overlooking that part of the Adriatic Sea placed between Apulia and the Balkans called the Otranto Channel.

Precisely because of its location, every year at the turn of the year, the event "Dawn of Peoples" is organized, which we will talk about later.

Otranto is a small village of just 5,000 inhabitants, but in summer, it turns into a sort of "melting pot" of people from all corners of the globe.

Its ancient importance is evidenced by the fact that the Turks tried several times to take Otranto, succeeding only in 1480 and maintaining control for only one year, a year remembered by the population as terrible.

At the end of the long siege, after looting, violence, and killing, there remained only 800 survivors on whom conversion to Islam or death was imposed. These 800 survivors did not convert and were all killed. After the invaders were driven out, their bodies were moved to Otranto Cathedral.

A few centuries later they were declared martyrs by the church and became objects of worship because of this.

CATHEDRAL OF OTRANTO

The cathedral of Otranto is extraordinary. First of all, in terms of size, it is the largest church in Apulia, 54 meters long and 25 meters wide.

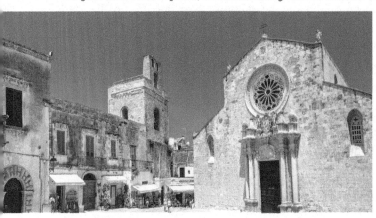

Suppose you pay attention to the columns that subdivide the cathedral space. In that case, you will notice something quite unusual: they are different in material type, color, and workmanship (some are smooth, others fluted). And the same goes for the capitals; no one is the same as another.

But what is most surprising is that instead of creating an environment composed of different pieces, the skillful arrangement of the columns managed to marry perfectly with the other elements of the cathedral, creating a just as much as surprising balance, both with the gilded coffered ceiling of the nave and with one of the most beautiful and mysterious mosaics ever created, dating back to the 12th century.

That mosaic occupies the entire length of the cathedral, with an interweaving of symbol motifs on whose interpretation scholars still disagree.

The mosaic is considered a true encyclopedia of medieval life; several events and characters are represented, all arranged in a balanced and unified whole. The sight of it cannot help but leave one amazed and incredulous. It also imparts a sense of disquiet precisely because of the mysteries concealed in it, along with a sense of horror vacui precisely because of its decorative fullness. An incredible treasure of Puglia's historical-artistic heritage.

Among the apses, the left one preserves in some cases the remains of those who the Turks killed in 1480.

HISTORIC CENTER AND HARBOR

The old town, where the harbor is included, is a maze of small streets and lanes with craft stores and restaurants. This was once one of the most important harbors and landings for ships from the east. You have to imagine the constant comings and goings of goods and people from all over the known world, with merchant ships leaving and arriving, the various sighting and defense systems (the towers), given the constant threat from the Turks.

THE CASTLE

Because of its strategic location, Otranto has a castle with a system of ramparts and defensive walls that, if they once served to repel enemies, today lend themselves to being places where visitors can touch history and enjoy the beauty and atmosphere of this magnificent seaside village.

The cartel's moats have also become venues for demonstrations and events, while ancient bombards are preserved and can be observed in its courtyard.

BAUXITE QUARRY

Before talking about the beautiful Otranto coastline, just a few kilometers from the city, there is a unique place, the bauxite quarry.

Bauxite was extracted from this quarry for several decades, until the activity was later discontinued. So far, nothing special.

With time, however, thanks to the limestone terrain and the presence of groundwater, the quarry is transformed into a small lake environment in front of which you cannot remain impassive. The spectacle is given by the strong contrast between the deep red of the quarry walls and the emerald color of the water, to which is added the green of the surrounding nature, has slowly reclaimed the territory.

An exceptional place, where at times it seems to be on another planet, a must-visit.

THE BEACHES OF OTRANTO

Let us now talk about what can be considered a paradise on earth: the beaches of Otranto. Actually, the entire Salento coast, both Ionian and Adriatic, can be considered a paradise.

However, let us start with Otranto and its beautiful beaches:

BAIA DEI TURCHI

The name comes from the Turks landing here during the siege OF 1480.

The beach is ideal for those who love contact with nature, which can be reached by walking along the paths of a dense pine forest. The beach is free and characterized by very white sand;

BEACH OF ALIMINI

The name of this beach, not far from the Bay of Turks, is due to the nearby presence of the Alimini lakes.

The sand here is golden, and in addition to the free beach, there are also lidos and kiosks;

BEACH OF MULINO D'ACQUA

The main feature of this beach is the different shades of blue of the waters. In addition, the entire beach is surrounded by caves and rocks.

The best-known cave is Grotta Sfondata, inside which it forms a natural basin that can be accessed from the sea;

BEACH OF RINULE

Fifteen meters of totally unspoiled, primeval beach surrounded by white limestone rocks. Crystal clear waters. You get there after some walking, but the beach spectacle is worth the effort.

BEACH OF PORTO BADISCO

A very renowned place in Otranto, where tourists can find beautiful coves with breathtaking views and wonderful SAND, with rocks plunging into the water. According to a legend, this is the landing place of Aeneas after escaping from Troy;

BAIA DELLE ORTE

This place is for lovers of calm, silence, and nature. Here glimpses of greenery and the presence of rocks give the idea of a wild place;

BEACH LA PUNTA

This area has well-equipped facilities to make the most of the deep blue sea. There are also renowned eateries ready to surprise your taste buds with typical local dishes;

BEACH TORRE DELL'ORSO

The beach is especially ideal for families with children. This place has won several awards for its waters and beauty. A pine forest surrounds a typically sandy beach with shallow waters.

L'ALBA DEI POPOLI

The event that takes place every year in Otranto is translated with "the dawn of the peoples."

It is now well known that Otranto is the easternmost city in Italy, and throughout its history, Otranto has always been a bridge between West and East. That is why a series of cultural events, concerts, art and film exhibitions, sports competitions, and many other events are organized between the months of December and January, in which all the cultures of the Mediterranean are called upon to participate in a mixture of history, culture and traditions.

This glorious event attracts thousands of tourists every year. The highlight is the event in front of the Punta Palascia lighthouse on the evening of December 31 to bid farewell to the old year and welcome the new one with the best of luck.

SALENTO COASTS

This is where the real problem of Salento arises: when we decide we want to go to the sea, having to choose the seaside location from more than 200 km of beaches, bays, inlets, coves, and cliffs is difficult. Nevertheless, no coastline can be said to be less beautiful or attractive than the others.

Before starting this trip to the Salento peninsula, the advice is to rent a car so you can move comfortably from one beach to another, even over several days.

THE SALENTO ADRIATIC COAST

We begin with the Adriatic coast, which we have already talked about with Ostuni and Otranto, so let us continue southward to the furthest edge, Santa Maria di Leuca, from which we will then ascend along the Ionian coast.

THE MARINAS OF MELENDUGNO

Halfway between Lecce and Otranto, a series of beaches are part of the Marina di Melendugno, which offer real postcard views: Torre dell'Orso, San Foca, Roca, Torre Sant'Andrea and Torre Specchia Ruggeri constitute a mind-blowing spectacle.

1. San Foca is first in order, where in the harbor, you can admire an ancient watchtower dating back to the 1500s, and the Grotta degli Amanti, where according to legend, two lovers sought shelter. Then, especially on a clear day, it is possible to catch a glimpse of the Albanian mountains on the horizon. A sight not to be missed.

2. Roca Vecchia is another area that exerts a strong attraction for tourists, where nature and history come together: here, in fact, we have the enchanting Cave of Poetry, around which revolves the legend of a princess who loved to dive right here and where poets used to come to look for the girl to make her the muse of their poetic compositions.

3. Torre dell'Orso is among the most popular destinations in Salento, with white beaches and a crystal-clear sea embraced by a fragrant pine forest. In Torre dell'Orso, you can visit the Grotto of San Cristoforo, where graffiti is of considerable archaeological value. Making this beach famous are two stacks called "The Two Sisters." **Legend tells of two sisters who were enchanted by the beauty of the place; however, they drowned there while bathing. They were precisely turned into stacks so that they could admire the beauty of Torre dell'Orso for eternity.**

4. Torre Sant Andrea, on the other hand, is a popular destination for younger people who can enjoy concerts and find many clubs here.

The coast here is rocky and rugged, with caves and ravines interspersed with coves, with clear water that sometimes takes on cobalt-colored features.

SANTA CESAREA TERME

A visit to Santa Cesarea Terme is not to be disdained at all. In fact, although there are no beaches here, it is possible to admire the many villas and aristocratic palaces built by wealthy bourgeoisie as vacation spots. Since the early 1900s, this has been a bathing and vacation destination.

In addition, as the name of the village says, there is a spa, where I am sure you will appreciate a stop.

They are located inside an old building, now equipped with all modern conveniences. From four underground caves flow these waters, whose beneficial qualities have been known for 500 years.

ZINZULUSA CAVE

Continuing further south, halfway between Santa Cesarea Terme and Castro, there is one of the most scenically and geologically beautiful and interesting caves in the world: the Grotta Zinzulusa.

It can be accessed by sea. It is 160 meters long and is divided into three environ-

ments: the first is the "Conca," from which you access the "Corridor of Wonders," so called because the stalactites and stalagmites that characterize it with their different shapes have caused the inhabitants of nearby places to give each of these elements a name that recalls various objects and figures. In the corridor, there is also a small lake, called "Trabocchetto," followed by the most spectacular environment of this small geological complex: the "Crypt," a 25-meter-high room where the large and mighty columns give the place the appearance of a cathedral. Added to this environment is the Cocito Pond, which offers the sight of pure water on the surface and brackish water on the bottom, inhabited by microorganisms.

The name of the cave comes from an old legend:

Apparently, near the cave lived a very evil rich man, the Baron of Castro, who required his daughter to dress only in rags (zinzuli in the local dialect). One day, a fairy brought the little girl a new dress while the old rags were carried away by the wind and petrified on the cave walls, which took precisely the name Grotta della Zinzulusa . On the other hand, the Baron was thrown into the Cocito Lake, where the crustaceans remained blind forever after witnessing the scene. ✎

Visiting the cave only with an authorized guide and after paying a ticket is possible.

A little tip: exactly where you start to visit the Zinzulusa Cave, there is a mooring with boats to visit the other nearby caves as well. Of particular beauty is the Blue Cave, where there is a great play of light.

CASTRO

Not far away is the small town of Castro, once an episcopal seat and with some importance, as evidenced by the presence of a mighty castle and a large cathedral in the historic center located in the upper part.

The lower part, or Castro Marina, has a very cozy little harbor where you can let the gentle breeze sway you while sipping a cool drink.

Castro has no beaches, the coast is rocky, and its waters are particularly high. Therefore, it is not a suitable place to visit with children with you. However, a small gem not far from Castro is the "Cala

dell'Acquaviva." It is inland thanks to lush vegetation surrounding the small beach, ready to show itself in all its beauty. A steep cliff bounds it, creating an exceptional environment, where the presence of cold water makes one think of a Norwegian fjord.

Despite its wild yet enchanting appearance, the Acquaviva cove is well equipped, and it is highly recommended to stop for a few hours to relax in this superb place.

CIOLO BRIDGE

We are now at the most extreme part of the peninsula, and before we reach the final point, we can pause at another interesting place, the "Ciolo Bridge."

There is a breathtaking view from this 60-meter-high bridge: the area is a canyon created by the erosive action of water and wind and is a wonderful example of Mediterranean scrub vegetation.

A few daredevils have even dived from the 60-meter height of the bridge, which is recommended not to do, both because of the danger of jumping into the void below which the seabed is rocky, and because it is forbidden.

This area is full of caves, used by many birds that find shelter there. Below the bridge, there is also a small beach you can access by a flight of steps nearby, from where you can see the bridge and the rocks on which it stands from below.

SANTA MARIA DI LEUCA

Finally, we come to the far end of Puglia and the Salento peninsula, Santa Maria di Leuca.

The southernmost point of the entire region (the common belief is that the Ionian and Adriatic seas touch here; in reality, such contact occurs near Otranto), where according to some sources, St. Peter landed from Palestine to begin evangelization of the local peoples.

Santa Maria di Leuca is wonderful for its coastline, where sand and rocks alternate, and its splendid caves and seabed, attracting thousands of divers every year.

Conversely, the hinterland sees a continuous succession of villas and palaces reflecting different styles, which gently slope down to the sea.

On the highest and most scenic point rises a shrine, which can be reached from below by walking up 184 steps.

Along the steps runs a 120-meter waterfall, a reminder of the great feat of constructing the Apulian aqueduct (a critical infrastructure for a water-poor region like Apulia). Here are the terminal works of this impressive structure that spans the entire area.

Having taken the 184 steps, one arrives at the Santa Maria Finibus Terrae shrine, according to tradition blessed by St. Peter himself, and a gateway to paradise. The sanctuary stands on an ancient temple dedicated to the goddess Minerva, so much so that some evidence is still visible inside the church.

The lighthouse stands not far from the shrine, nearly 50 meters high and rising 102 meters above sea level.

For an unparalleled panoramic view, one must climb the 254 steps. But the strenuous climb is worth it: once at the top, a magnificent 360- degree view is there, ready to amaze anyone. To add to the fascination, watching the sunset from the top of the lighthouse is one of the most beautiful experiences you will ever have in your life. The play of light created by the interaction between the sun's rays as it sets on the horizon and the sea steals the beholder's heart.

Both with respect to the east and west of Santa Maria di Leuca, there are several caves, which you can visit with guided boat excursions: Grotta Porcinara, Grotta del Diavolo, Grotta dei Giganti, Grotta del Bambino, Grotta delle Tre Porte, and many others, each with unique stories and anecdotes that are well worth a visit.

WEST COAST OF SALENTO

After enjoying the beauty of the extreme tip of Puglia, we continue to its east coast, the Ionian coast.

MARINA DI PESCOLUSE

Going up, you immediately come across the area that has been dubbed the "Maldives of Salento," the marina of Pescoluse.

A blue and calm sea, very white beach dunes and thick vegetation surrounding the 4 km of beach make this location a real corner of paradise on earth. Here portions of free beaches alternate with private lidos, plus the resort is particularly suitable for families with children.

The town of Pescoluse is not very big, but it has all the necessary services for vacationers, while in the evening it is transformed thanks to an extremely lively movida with bars, restaurants, clubs where you can dance and have fun.

Pescoluse is absolutely one of those destinations that you cannot forget after you have been there.

GALLIPOLI

Among the most popular places in recent years, especially by younger people, is Gallipoli.

With its clubs, nightlife, events, and beaches, Gallipoli fills up with thousands of vacationers every summer, who cannot help but be amazed by this location.

Gallipoli is not only beaches and fun, but like many other places in Salento it is also culture, history, traditions. So here is that a visit to the old part, located on an island, is an excellent idea. The stars of the old town are the Angevin castle and the basilica of St. Agatha.

In all the old part there are as many as 17 churches and monasteries, connected by secret tunnels, some of which lead outside the walls of the old town.

Also here, as in other areas of Salento, the Baroque has characterized the physiognomy of churches and towns.

One example is the church of Santa Maria della Purità, where along- side the rich Baroque ornaments and precious paintings, a beautiful majolica floor can be admired.

GALLIPOLI BEACHES

Spiaggia della purità

There is one at the foot of the old town, called the purity beach, a quiet place to relax, with imposing defensive walls behind it;

Baia Verde

A trendy beach in Gallipoli, where private lidos to stretches of free beach meet everyone's needs.

The beach is characterized by wonderful sand, surrounded by Mediterranean scrub, ready to inebriate the senses with its colors and smells. Adding further value to the place is the placid sea with its crystal-clear waters, which at every sunset offers a dreamlike spectacle.

The beach is only 3 km from the center and is easily accessible both on foot and by public transportation;

Spiaggia Degli Innamorati

Further south of Baia Verde is "Lovers' Beach," in the "LI Foggi" area. One is within the Regional Natural Park of the Island of St. Andrew and Punta Pizzo coastline. The beach's name comes from the fact that the place is quiet and uncrowded.

The beach is characterized by fine, cream-colored sand with a turquoise sea. It is truly a heavenly place where you can leave behind the daily hustle and bustle of the city and enjoy a moment of total relaxation together with a few intimates with whom to share peace and serenity.

The beach is reached after a short walk through the Mediterranean maquis, with its smells and aromas.

It is worth mentioning that the lovers' beach, or as the locals call it, "Foggi" beach, is located within a protected area known as the "Regional Natural Park of Sant'Andrea Island and Punta Izzo," considered the green lung of Salento. From a biodiversity point of view, the area is held in very high regard. The protected area has large expanses of woodland, with very special flora and fauna. At least ten species of oak trees have been counted in this area.

The area closest to the sea turns into a lush pine forest with rare plants and shrubs.

PUNTA DELLA SUINA

If with the marina of Pescoluse we were talking about the Maldives, with the beach of Punta della Suina, we are talking instead about the Caribbean.

So-called because of the particular projection of the shoreline towards the sea, this stretches alternate between sand and areas with rocks where you can dive.

What is wonderful are the crystal-clear sea, able to hypnotize you with its reflections, and the hinterland with its pine forest full of scents and smells.

A little further on is Punta Izzo, another must-see destination.

PORTO SELVAGGIO

Continuing further, there is a hidden place, one of the most beautiful in Italy and one of the most magical in all of Apulia and the Salento coast: Porto Selvaggio.

This enchanting place is located within the natural park of the same name, where out of 432 hectares of coastline, as many as 268 are composed of wooded area due to reforestation of the area.

The small cove that gives its name to the whole area is surrounded by a frame of rocks and ravines from which it is possible to dive, while the beach looks like pebbly sand. Because of the nearby presence of a spring that can be reached by swimming, if you do not fear the cold, a stream of fresh, cold water has been created in the cove.

Walking along one of the forest paths that protects this little gem, we arrive at Uluzzo Bay, where there is a Paleolithic deposit with stone artifacts and even the remains of large animals that once inhabited this area.

Continuing along such paths, one comes across several caves, such as "Capelvenere," a name given to a fern seedling, within which ancient evidence from different eras has been found.

Among the many routes, one leads up to the "Torre dell'Alto," an imposing Aragonese fortification now home to the marine biology museum. This museum fortification stands on a point where its tip, which is 50 meters overhanging the sea, is called "Dirupo della Dannata." Here, a young woman sought death to escape the evil Count Giangerolamo Acquaviva.

The whole area of Porto Selvaggio is full of treasures and beauties, emotions to be discovered and experienced. Even the place that seems most mundane hides priceless treasures.

PORTO CESAREO

On the journey along the Ionian coast, a next stop is a place whose beaches are reminiscent of the Caribbean: Porto Cesareo. This destination is also among the most popular in Salento.

Porto Cesareo's beaches run uninterrupted for 17 km, with a calm sea with shallow sandy bottoms.

In front of the town's beach, about 200 meters offshore, are several islets, the largest known as "L'isola dei Conigli," which can be reached by boat or walking. The seabed, never more than a meter deep, allows this original "walk" to the islets. It should be remembered, however, that these strips of land are protected areas, and it is necessary to respect the laws for the protection of these natural environments, should one decide to visit them.

Two hamlets of Porto Cesareo deserve to be mentioned: "Torre Chianca" and "Torre Lapillo."

- Torre Chianca is considered ideal for going diving. Its seabed is incredible. Moreover, it is also possible to observe some columns from the Roman era "anchored" to the seabed following the shipwreck of the ship that transported them.
- Torre Lapillo, on the other hand, is characterized by free beaches alternating with private beaches. Thanks to the presence of services and facilities, it is possible to carry out one of the many activities offered.

Also part of the municipality of Porto Cesareo is the beach of Punta Prosciutto.

This beach, precisely because of its beauty, is known worldwide, and tourists come from everywhere to enjoy the unique beauty of this place.

It is composed of 2 km of a very white beach, with the sea touching all shades of blue and azure.

Precisely because of its beauty and to preserve flora and fauna, it became necessary to create an institutional body and give birth to the "Count Marsh Regional Nature Park."

SMALL JOURNEY INTO SALENTO'S PREHISTORY: DOLMENS

After exploring the majestic beauty of the Salento coast, let's see how the equally magnificent hinterland holds something very special: dolmens.

But what are dolmens?

Dolmens are structures dating back to prehistoric times, consisting of large stone slabs placed vertically to support a large horizontal slab. On their functions, it is speculated that they were probably tombs or structures to perform rituals. Apulia is among the regions with the largest number of dolmens, most of which are in Salento (it is estimated there were at least 100 at one time, today, there are many fewer).

So, while delighting in all that this land has to offer, why not set out in search of these ancient structures that have been here for millennia and seem to guard the land?

These are the main dolmens that can be visited:

- The "Megalithic Garden of Italy": in Giurdignano, a small town near Otranto, there is a large area to protect and preserve seven dolmens, each of them with their peculiarities. Local authorities provide a series of tours, even at night so that you can visit them by bike or if you want, even by carriage.
- Within the Cultural Park of the Dolmen "Li Scusi" is placed the eponymous Dolmen, among the largest in the region, 1 meter high and with as many as 8 boulders supporting the horizontal slab. It was the first dolmen found in Apulia in 1879.
- The "Argentina" and "Così Così" dolmens, a few kilometers from Santa Maria di Leuca: the former is in an excellent state of preservation. At the same time, the latter is known because fragments of terracotta and bone remains have been found. The two dolmens, "Plau Grande Caroppo I" and "Plau Piccolo Caroppo II," located in Corigliano d'Otranto, are fascinating. The former has a gallery structure consisting of nine pillars supporting the horizontal slab, while the latter is smaller.
- The dolmen "Chianca Santo Stefano" in Carpignano Salentino has a structure that differs considerably from other dolmens in Salento, similar to those in northern Europe and consisting of three slabs.
- The dolmens "Placa" and "Gurgulante" are located along the road to Calimera in Melendugno. The former features seven vertical pillars and a roof, while the latter has a height of 90 cm.
- The dolmens "Stabile" and "Ore" are in Giuggianello. The structure of "Stabile" is still strong and consists of 2 monoliths and 7 columns, formed by overlapping boulders. On the other hand, that of the "Ore" dolmen consists of a monolithic and 2 stacked masses of stones, all resting on a rocky base.

MELPIGNANO AND THE TARANTA FESTIVAL

The event that every self-respecting Salento resident waits for at the end of August is the Night of the Taranta. A riot of celebration, dancing, music, and sounds where a small town, Melpignano, becomes the meeting center of cultures from all over the world. Hundreds of thousands of people meet to dance to the rhythm of the "pizzica," a typical Salento dance, under a huge stage. International artists participating in this event of celebration and communion between cultures.

But where does all this come from?

The "pizzica" is a type of dance that probably has its roots in the festivals honoring the Greek god Dionysus, in which moral restrictions were relaxed, and people threw themselves into wild singing and dancing.

Following the advent of Christianity, the Greek god was replaced with St. Paul, a healer saint who was often invoked in the various songs accompanying the traditional music, mainly performed with tambourine, accordion, violin and violin and guitar.

But what were the song and music supposed to heal from? From the bite of the tarantula, "taranta" in the local dialect.

Working in the fields it was easy for peasants to be bitten by the tarantula, which is why it was believed that such songs had the thaumaturgic power to nullify the power of the spider's venom.

Born therefore from a local belief, part of the traditions of Salento, today the pizzica finds its highest expression on the night of the Taranta of Melpignano, where it is reworked and combined with other musical genres to give life to an

incredible spectacle, in which for a whole night people sing and dance throughout the town in an almost surreal atmosphere, where ancient and modern merge, where the reverence for tradition also coexists with the impetus towards the future, with the awareness and the desire to never leave behind the history of this wonderful tradition.

FOODS TO ABSOLUTELY ENJOY IN SALENTO

Pasticciotto leccese: a small oval pastry cupcake filled with custard. In Salento, it is traditional to eat it for breakfast, probably because there is no better way to start the day.

There is also an alternative version, called "fruttone," where the pasticciotto is filled with almond paste and jam, all covered in dark chocolate.

Rustico leccese: two puff pastry disks between mozzarella, béchamel, and tomato. Some variations also include pepper and nutmeg. Best enjoyed hot if possible. A joy for the palate.

Friselle: made from durum wheat, frisella is cooked twice to obtain a porous and firm appearance. It is very hard, so before being seasoned with salt, oil, and tomatoes, it must be softened by "soaking" it in water.

When you bite into a frisella, you feel Salento in your mouth and all of Puglia.

Pettole: small globs of leavened dough, fried in oil, crispy outside and soft inside. Accompanied by different side dishes depending on the area: vincotto, salted anchovies, pieces of cod, or half-cooked broccoli - a delight.

Fish: Fish is also very good in Salento, in whatever way you cook it, whether fried or roasted, with sauce or in soup. In particular, mullet is to be tasted.

The wine production of Salento is also characterized by the excellent, whose demand is constantly expanding.

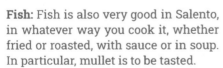

Primitivo di Manduria: it is believed that it was the Greeks who brought this type of wine over 2000 years ago, and today it is among the most famous wines of Puglia.

Its color is very deep red, almost purplish, with a sustained aroma of red fruits with a full and harmonious flavor.

Negroamaro: perhaps the best-selling Apulian wine in the world. Negroamaro red has a very dark color, and a lingering taste with a slightly bitter aftertaste. Excellent with meat and aged cheeses.

Negroamaro rosé, on the other hand, is widely used to give substance to other local wines.

Leverano: white wine with a straw yellow color, very delicate and dry. Perfect for appetizers. Its grapes are harvested in the early morning hours and undergo decanting and fermentation at low temperatures.

CHAPTER 6

TARANTO AND PROVINCIA

With the last beaches mentioned earlier, we arrived near one of the most important cities in the region, Taranto. Here we are at the point where Murgia and Salento territories meet. A few kilometers from the magnificent beaches here, it is possible to find rock churches and dwellings carved into the rocks in canyons. It is no coincidence that here we have the "Parco delle Gravine," a protected area where it is possible to see entire settlements and villages built in the ravines, in territories that are impervious and beautiful at the same time.

TARANTO

Taranto is a city of Greek origin, more precisely it was founded by Spartan exiles (the only colony founded by the Lacedaemonian population). Because of its strategic location, the fertility of its soils, and its propensity for trade, Taranto has always been an important city that has had its own influence on all of southern Italy and beyond.

Today the city is home to one of the largest steel mills in Europe.

Taranto is also called "the city of two seas" as it precisely overlooks two seas, the "Mar Grande" and the "Mar Piccolo," which form the Gulf of Taranto.

"MarTA"

To learn about the history of Taranto and beyond and to understand its prestige in past centuries, one must visit the "MarTA," Taranto's museum, one of the most important in Italy. In this museum one can trace the entire history of the area from the Stone Age to the city's splendor during the Hellenistic age.

The museum is well organized and interesting, combining fun with knowledge. It is not only limited to introducing the history of Taranto, but depending on the period in which you visit it, you can see valuable paintings from different periods. In addition, temporary exhibitions and activities are often organized that can actively bring the museum experience to life.

HISTORIC CENTER

Another feature of Taranto is its historic center, which sits on an island. Were it not for two bridges (one revolving, another thing to see), it would be detached from the modern part of the city.

It is precisely this "isolation," according to those who have seen it and experienced it, that makes the old part of Taranto a world apart, where every stone seems to have so much to tell, and where around every corner there is either an incredible glimpse or a wonderful view.

The streets here are so narrow that one person can only walk some at a time. One street that perfectly testifies to this peculiarity is called "Street of the Kiss" because two people cannot pass without touching each other.

This narrow conformation of the streets in the old town is due to essentially defensive reasons, given the constant attacks by Saracens in the

Middle Ages, which led at one point to the destruction of the city and its necessary reconstruction.

CATHEDRAL OF SAN CATALDO

Entering the historic center, you must recognize the Cathedral of San Cataldo, the oldest in Apulia. Built about the middle of the 10th century, it was built on the ruins of a pre-existing religious building, possibly dating back about two centuries earlier. The building has undergone several changes over time: the original Byzantine-style layout underwent some renovations in the 11th century, while the Baroque-style facade was added in the 1700s. The old Norman bell tower no longer exists, having been destroyed by an earthquake around 1450. The church's interior consists of three naves, one central and two side aisles, and holds the tombs of some of the most important figures in Taranto's history.

THE ARAGONESE CASTLE

Along with the cathedral, also dominating the historic center, is the Aragonese castle, called "Castel Sant'Angelo," located at the far corner of the historic center island. Built-in Byzantine times around 900 AD, the rectangular-plan castle was originally designed to repel attacks by the Venetians and Syracusans, with tall, soaring towers to hurl arrows, stones, and boiling oil at enemies. In the late 1400s, King Ferdinand of Aragon II had the castle enlarged and modified, adding seven towers, including the Rivellino- a tower separated from the main part of the structure to allow a protected exit route in case of siege-giving it the appearance that can be seen today.

THE GREEK COLUMNS

Among the few remaining vestiges in the historic center of Greek Taranto are the two columns left standing in the ruins of an ancient temple. As soon as you cross the swing bridge from the modern city, these columns seem to be there waiting for the tourist to tell of millennia of history and the great prestige that Taranto held in antiquity.

Old Taranto is teeming with ancient hidden treasures that deserve to be discovered, hoping to avoid getting stuck in the narrow streets.

REMAINS OF GREEK TARANTO

Throughout the city, several sites testify to its Greek origins: from the necropolis, where 160 tombs can be visited, to the archaeological park of Collepasso, a true open-air museum, where it is possible to see the remains of a wall defending the city and a necropolis with different types of burials.

THE GULF OF TARANTO AND THE LEGEND OF THE SIRENS

Walking along Taranto's waterfront and observing its beautiful gulf, in some stretches, one cannot help but admire statues depicting mermaids built of marine concrete to resist the water's erosive action. The presence of these mermaids, which further embellish an enchanting landscape in itself, conceals an exciting romantic story.

In the days of Greek Taranto, sirens were so captivated by the beauty of the gulf that they decided to build their underwater castle here.

A young couple lived in the village: she was a beautiful girl who, due to his constant absence from her job as a fisherman, succumbed to the flattery of a local nobleman.

Gripped with guilt, she confessed everything to her husband, who decided to take her to sea and drown her in the gulf waters. However, the mermaids saved the girl, who, given her beauty, crowned her their queen with the name Skuma (Foam).

The young man, however, regretting what he had done, returned after some time to the scene of the misdeed, weeping all his tears. Here the sirens brought him before their queen. She forgave her husband and convinced the sirens not to kill him and bring him back to the surface.

The boy, however, decided he wanted his wife with him again, and with the help of a fairy, he managed to take her away from the mermaids' castle. ❧

At this point, the legend has two different endings: in one, the Jovans returned to shore and lived happily ever after; in the other ending, a gigantic wave swept over the boy and the mermaids, disappearing into thin air, while the beautiful girl out of grief became a nun and locked herself up in what is now called "Monacella Tower" in the Aragonese castle.

THE PROCESSION OF THE MYSTERIES

After this brief legendary interlude, I want to talk about a particular event held during Holy Week, the procession of the mysteries.

The procession of the mysteries is a type of event designed to commemorate the passion and resurrection of Jesus. It is generally celebrated on the evening of the Thursday or Friday before Easter, somewhat throughout southern Italy. However, in Taranto, it takes on special connotations: in its procession through the city center it even lasts 15 hours!

The whole event follows its particular iteration, where the brethren of the order of the Church of the Carmine wear a series of special garments: a white smock, a black belt, the rosary, the scapular (the symbol of the devotees of the Virgin of Mount Carmel), the cream- colored mozzetta, the black hat edged in blue lowered onto the shoulders, and the white hood lowered onto the face. They are all barefoot and carry on their shoulders a series of statues depicting the last hours of Jesus' life.

What stands before one's eyes is something unique, where one cannot help but be fascinated and disquieted simultaneously. Participants in the procession walk at a very slow pace, called "nazzicata."

Attending this kind of religious event is a mystical experience, regardless of whether one is a believer. It isn't easy to describe what one can experience in this example of popular devotion that has its roots several centuries back.

RAVINES NATURAL PARK

Traveling through the beauty of the Murgia territory, we saw how entire complexes of caves were used as dwellings and more, how these cavities within the limestone lent themselves to human activity, and how more than one civilization flourished in these areas that at first glance may appear impervious and inhospitable.

The greatest concentration of ravines is in the province of Taranto, so much so that a few years ago, the "Gravine Natural Park" was established, an area that involves several inhabited centers and aims to protect and promote knowledge of this territory, where the wildest nature with its very rich biodiversity and human ingenuity coexist, capable of building centers clinging along the ridges of these ravines, which resist modernity and keep intact the charm of past civilizations.

As many as 13 municipalities located in the province of Taranto are part of this area: Castellaneta, Massafra, Crispiano, Palagianello, Ginosa, Grottaglie, Palagiano, Laterza, Martina Franca, Montemesola, Mottola, San Marzano di San Giuseppe and Statte; one municipality, however, Villa Castelli, is in the province of Brindisi.

Most of these centers are located not coincidentally not far from Matera, where we have the city carved out of stones par excellence.

The surprising thing is that each of these villages preserves priceless relics related to the rock civilizations that inhabited these canyons carved by the erosive action of water.

The village of Grottaglie already has in its toponym the idea of a multitude of caves in its territory. In particular, outside the center, it is possible to take a walk in the Riggio ravine, where there is a natural waterfall at the foot of which a truly impressive lake forms. In the Fantiano quarries, on the other hand, it is possible to walk among towers of tuffs excavated by the hand of man thousands of years ago, with nature taking over these places once abandoned by man. To date, the area has undergone reclamation to the extent that shows and events are organized.

Massafra has a canyon known as the Gravina of San Marco, which even cuts the town in two, inside which you can see the ancient caves inhabited by man since ancient times.

There are some perfectly preserved cave churches here, such as the church of San Leonardo (with frescoes dating back to the 11th-12th centuries), or the church of Candlemas, topped by domes, each with its particular shape. The columns still have their decorated capitals, while a Madonna painted in a typically Byzantine style stands out among the frescoes.

It is also possible to observe the hermit monk's cell near the church.

Very spectacular is the ravine of the "Madonna della Scala," which can be accessed after descending a long flight of steps immersed in the most impervious nature. Continuing, one arrives instead at another mystical and magical place: the pharmacy of the Magician Greguro, no less than 12 interconnected caves with over 200 niches in which the magician is believed to have prepared medicinal herbs.

From the magnificent medieval village of Mottola, one can visit an entire rock village called "Petruscio," built apparently in the 9th century AD by inhabitants fleeing from the Saracens. The peculiarity of Petruscio is the 600 caves arranged on several floors as if they were skyscrapers.

The element that stands out the most, so much so that it has been called the "Sistine of rock civilization," is the church of San Nicola, so called because of the valuable paintings contained inside, some of which, such as the crucifixion on the facade, is among the oldest in the entire region.

Perhaps the most striking ravine is that of Castellaneta: it is up to 300 meters wide, reaches 140 meters deep and stretches for 10 km. It can be seen in its entirety from the belvedere in the town's center. Something majestic, in front of which you cannot help but remain mute and appreciate its beauty.

An experienced guide is required to visit it, as accessing it is not easy.

The other ravine that must be visited is that of Laterza: the special place is the "Cantina Spagnola," an underground church. It is attested that a chivalric order was born in the 1600s, traces of which are on the walls, where a whole cycle of stories related to this order is frescoed, with still many obscure points. Finally, the church of San Lorenzo also has some very interesting elements.

FOODS TO ABSOLUTELY ENJOY IN AND AROUND TARANTO

Like the other areas of the region, Taranto and its province have a lot to offer from a gastronomic point of view. One is spoiled for choice between what the sea offers and what the hinterland offers.

Tarantine-style mussels: one of the specialties of Taranto, a major center for mussel farming.

Taranto-style mussels have a strong, bold flavor. Cooked in a pan with chili pepper and tomato and a crouton of bread to dip in the sauce. An incredible delicacy.

Clementine: in the province of Taranto are grown these very sweet mandarins, in whose segments, unlike other types of mandarins, there are no seeds.

Clementines are also considered a prized quality because of the area's sunny climate. They are still harvested by hand (between September and December) to avoid spoiling the fruit. The authenticity of these products of the earth never goes out of style.

Roast meat: throughout the province of Taranto, there are rotisseries ready to let you taste an incredible variety of meat specialties. Roulades, chops, ribs, sausages, you name it.

The meat is cooked over wood in stoves fit for the purpose, thanks to the skill of the rotisserie workers, who are adept at understanding how strong the fire is and how to place the different varieties of meat on the stove to ensure that they cook to the right point and do not burn.

The roasted meat that arrives on the table is an absolutely indescribable explosion of flavors. All are accompanied by local bread and wine.

As for the wines of Taranto and the province, one wine in particular should be mentioned.

Le Colline ioniche tarantine: a white wine, straw-yellow in color of varying intensity, sometimes with amber highlights; it has a very delicate and pleasant aroma with floral and fruity notes. This wine is also produced in red and rosé versions.

FINAL WORDS

My dear reader,

I hope this book has given you a foretaste of the beautiful trip you may be taking to Puglia very soon.

After reading about all the wonders this region has to offer, I think you will now fully agree with what I anticipated at the beginning of this book: it is indeed a tough task to choose what to visit in the short time of a stay in Puglia!

To help you in this, I would like to remind you that I am at your complete disposal in case you need help in planning your trip. If you wish, you can visit my website **myfriendpetru.com** and contact me.

I will be very happy to meet you and help you create a perfect tour for you!

Also, if you'd like, please leave a review for this book!

It would help me improve my content and allow me to further my book writing business!

I thank you for reading this guidebook that I have created with the intention of telling the story of Puglia to those who do not yet know it, and I hope to meet you soon to experience beautiful Puglia adventures together!

A warm hug,
Francesco, your Apulian friend.

FOLLOW ME

ON SOCIAL MEDIA

@petru.life

@petru.life

@petru - Francesco Giampetruzzi

Made in the USA
Coppell, TX
17 April 2024